MARKETING
TO AMERICAN
LATINOS

About the Author

 **Isabel Valdés,** a native of Chile and an American by choice, has been a leader in researching the Hispanic market in the United States. As founder and president of Hispanic Market Connections, Inc., she has been a pioneer in multicultural research. In 1998 she was named president of Cultural Access Worldwide, a subsidiary of Access Worldwide. Recently, she became the chairperson of Cultural Access Worldwide, in order to pursue her interests in teaching and writing.

Ms. Valdés is frequently called on to share her expertise with a long list of clients, including Procter & Gamble, Kraft, Nabisco, General Mills, Coca-Cola, Goya Foods, Pepsi-Cola, AT&T, Pacific Bell, Honda of America, American Airlines, Time Warner, Children's Television Workshop, Universal Studios, Florida Tourism, Disneyland, Chase Manhattan Bank, Bank One, Bank of America, Monterey Bay Aquarium, Coors, Tecate and many others.

ACNielsen selected Valdés to help build a Hispanic panel for its Homescan™ service in Los Angeles. She has also developed standardized testing and language segmentation techniques.

Ms. Valdés is a lecturer and faculty member at Stanford University's Professional Publishing Course and at UCLA's Anderson School of Business Executive Education Program. She co-founded the research committee for the Association of Hispanic Advertising Agencies (AHAA) and co-founded the Ethnic Research Committee of the Advertising Research Foundation (ARF). She frequently speaks about the Latino market to audiences in the U.S. and abroad.

PART 1

MARKETING TO AMERICAN LATINOS

A Guide to the In-Culture Approach

M. Isabel Valdés

PARAMOUNT MARKET PUBLISHING, INC.

Paramount Market Publishing, Inc.
301 S. Geneva Street, Suite 109
Ithaca, NY 14850
www.paramountbooks.com
Telephone: 607-275-8100; 888-787-8100   Facsimile: 607-275-8101

Publisher: James Madden
Editorial Director: Doris Walsh

Copyright © 2000
First published USA 2000

This publication is designed to provide accurate and authoritative information in regard to the subject matter covered. It is sold with the understanding that the publisher is not engaged in rendering legal, accounting, or other professional services. If legal advice or other expert assistance is required, the services of a competent professional should be sought.

Library of Congress Catalog Number:
Cataloging in Publication Data available
ISBN 0-9671439-3-4

Book design and composition: Paperwork

CONTENTS

FOREWORD

HOW TO USE THIS BOOK

Paramount Market Publishing, Inc. is pleased to be at the forefront of multimedia publishing. At the back of *Marketing to American Latinos, Part 1* you will a CD-ROM.

Get your individual passcode for access to the book's web site by calling us at the toll-free number below. On the site you will find music, photographs, a slide show, and additional material that is not included in the book. The author, Isabel Valdés, has generously granted copyright permission to all book buyers so that they may use tables and charts from the web site in their own presentations. They are in a .pdf format so that they may be easily downloaded. They should always be appropriately credited.

On the CD-ROM you will also find many of the television advertisements cited in the case studies as well as photographs, charts, and tables from the book.

Please enjoy browsing through the web site. If you want to study tables and charts you will probably want to refer to the book. If you need to put charts and tables into a presentation, you can usually find them on either the web site or on the CD-ROM. New sources and case materials will be added to the web site on a regular basis.

FOR YOUR WEB SITE PASSCODE
1-888-787-8100

ACKNOWLEDGMENTS

Over the past five years, since my first book (*Hispanic Market Handbook*, Gale Research Publishers, 1995) was released, many readers from the business as well as the academic world, from the U.S. and abroad, gave me feedback about it, always in very positive terms. I wish to extend my thanks to them for their encouragement and feedback and for providing additional sources of information. I also want to thank those who by their constructive criticism contributed to the development of this book into the slimmer and more "user friendly" volume that you now hold.

I would like to give particular thanks to my colleagues Beth Broderson and Jennifer Lynch for their support and editorial direction in the development of the cyber version of this book (see http://www.access-cag.com and www.accesscag.com) and to Robert Douglas and Linda Stinchfield for making the cyber book a beautiful reality. Thanks to Gil Bugarin for the great graphs you created and to Elizabeth Von Radics for her copyediting help in earlier manuscripts.

To Jannet Torres, Jacqueline Gumucio, Isabel Balboa, Lady Delgado, David Morse and Liliana Caceres: Without your on-going support I would not have had the chance to study the Hispanic market and learn how to do it "In-Culture." *Gracias!*

This book is better than it might have been because of the editorial direction and suggestions of James J. Madden and Doris L. Walsh, my committed publishers at Paramount Market Publishing, Inc., who took the cyber version—which was created with an interactive mindset—and re-formatted it into this wonderful marketing book, in record time.

Special thanks to Aetna Life Insurance and Annuity Company for its generous support to launch the on-line version, and to Pueblo Corporation, with its *De Hispano a Hispano* services, for their underwriting of the national book launch and hence promoting it to the Hispanic marketing community. Also many, many thanks to *La Opinión*, *Latina* magazine and Access Worldwide Communications for partnering with me and helping make the book's national media launch a reality.

I wish to acknowledge my gratitude and appreciation to my dear friends, clients and colleagues who contributed case studies and data to illustrate how to execute In-Culture Hispanic marketing and advertising programs; Victoria Hudson, Monica Lozano, Willard Hill, Daisy Exposito, Hugo Pimienta, Norma and Hector Orci, Carl Kravetz, Federico Herrera, Christy Haubbeger, Cesar Melgoza, Horacio Gomes, Mathew Roth, Guillermo Paz, Manuel Fernandez, Meredith Spector, Kenneth Greenberg, Tom Maney, Alex Lopez Negrete, Lisa Skriloff, Tom Exter and Carlos Santiago.

Case studies were contributed by the following ad agencies specializing in Hispanic advertising: Cartel Creativo (San Antonio) with the Tecate, JCPenney and Paragon Cable case studies; cruz/kravetz:IDEAS (Los Angeles) with House Foods, California Lincoln Mercury Dealers Association and El Pollo Loco; Y&R/The Bravo Group (New York) with USPS's Dinero Seguro; and La Agencia de Orci y Asociados, (Los Angeles), Honda of America. *La Opinión*'s case study was contributed by its corporate management. Our partners, ACNielsen Hispanic Homescan Panel, and Geoscape contributed Hispanic purchase and market data, respectively.

Thank you all for helping make *Marketing to American Latinos* a true Hispanic marketing learning tool.

On my behalf and that of the U.S. Hispanic community, many thanks to the Ambassador of Spain in the United States, Don Antonio de Oyarzabal, who has opened a new cultural era between Latinos in the U.S. and *La Madre Patria*. Thanks for your on-going inspiration!

Finally, eternal thanks to my family, Julio Aranovich, my loving and patient spouse, and my children Gabriel and Clara. Your love and support keep me going, no matter what challenges I create. Thanks to my *madrina,* Dr. Celia Correas, who has been a lifelong role model and a friend, and to Loreto Caro Valdés, my "cyber niece" for her fresh inspiration and unconditional support. *Gracias!*

I truly hope this book brings you as many blessings as I have received working on it!

ISABEL VALDÉS
PALO ALTO, APRIL 2000

INTRODUCTION

Welcome to Hispanic Culture Marketing in the new millennium!

Preparing Part 1 of *Marketing to American Latinos: A Guide to the In-Culture Approach* has been a fascinating challenge for several reasons.

First, we enter the millennium with a positive balance sheet towards Hispanic marketing. After a decade of tangible bottom line results, most industries are already targeting Hispanic consumers and many now are beginning to recognize the power, and target, Hispanic businesses.

Second, Hispanic market growth is exponential and outpaced only by growth in Hispanic purchasing power. **Figure 0.1** shows that there were more and larger households in the market with even larger and faster growing incomes in 1999 than there were in 1990.

FIGURE 0.1

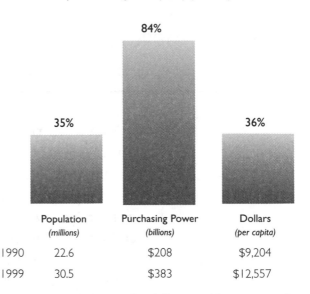

Growth Trends 1990–1999

Hispanic income gains outpace population growth.

	Population (millions)	Purchasing Power (billions)	Dollars (per capita)
1990	22.6	$208	$9,204
1999	30.5	$383	$12,557

Population: 35% Purchasing Power: 84% Dollars: 36%

Source: Selig Center for Economic Growth, University of Georgia, "Hispanic Buying Power by Place of Residence 1990-1999," Nov-Dec. 1998; and U.S. Census Bureau

Third, there are more reliable marketing data sources emerging and maturing. For example, the AC-Nielsen Homescan Panel tells us—almost real time—the volume of goods acquired by Hispanic households in many different categories and where this growing market segment goes shopping **(Figure 0.2)**.

FIGURE 0.2

Hispanic Shopping Behavior

Select Categories: What Do Hispanics Buy?

Buying Rate

	Non-Hispanic Market Households	Total Hispanic Households	ALL LANGUAGE SEGMENTS*		
			Spanish Only/Preferred	Bilingual	English Only/Preferred
Soft Drinks					
Carbonated	18.01	21.51	25.39	16.89	21.30
Low Calorie	19.98	12.90	6.45	15.47	17.26
Non-Carbonated	9.98	9.60	7.60	10.48	12.68
Powdered	6.80	5.52	4.92	6.45	4.77
Water (bottled)	8.08	7.27	5.17	8.77	9.01
Orange Juice (frozen)	8.93	7.79	6.07	9.60	9.00
Fruit Drinks (frozen)	3.74	7.17	8.17	5.72	8.85

* CAG's Language Segmentation

Source: ACNielsen Homescan, March-May Hispanic Consumer Panel, LA Market, 1999

Fourth, the magic of the Internet is bringing Hispanic consumers to cyberspace at an incredible rate. As I write, several Spanish-language Internet-based companies are growing by leaps and bounds, and many more are emerging. Even though U.S. Latinos trail behind non-Hispanic white households in computer ownership and literacy, computer penetration more than doubled between 1994 and 1998 **(Figure 0.3)**.

Finally, the massive success of Latinos in sports (Sammy Sosa, Oscar de la Hoya), film (Jennifer Lopez,

Salma Hayeck, Antonio Banderas, Edward James Olmos), film directors (Eduardo Navas, Cuis Valdez), music (Carlos Santana, Ricky Martin, Gloria Estefan, Shakira), writers (Isabel Allende), and media (Canales ñ, Fox Sports World Español, *Latina* magazine, *People en Español*) is just the beginning of what is to come.

This first part of *Marketing to American Latinos* is dedicated to "culture" and how to market in a "culturally attuned" manner (In-culture) to Hispanics. Since Latin culture is what binds us, Mexicans, Cubans, Puerto Ricans, Dominicans, Central and South Americans, either foreign-born or U.S.-born, understanding the culture is the main first step to successful Hispanic marketing.

Part 2 of the book, to be released in 2001, will cover issues related to media, Internet, business-to-business and, of course, Census 2000.

FIGURE 0.3

Hispanics Online

Computer ownership and subscription to Internet services for Hispanic households

- In 1994, only 13 percent of all Hispanic households had a computer in the home. In 1998, 30 percent of all Hispanic households owned a computer.

- In 1994, only 2 percent of Hispanic households were connected to the Internet. Today, 15 percent of all Hispanic households subscribe to Internet services.

- The rate of increase in computer-owning households by Hispanics is twice the national average.

- Hispanics tend to use the Internet for educational, informational, and e-mail purposes.

Source: The Tomas Rivera Policy Institute (TRPI), "Closing the Digital Divide: Enhancing Hispanic Participation in the Information Age," 1999

SECTION 1

THE "NEW" HISPANIC CONSUMER

Chapter 1

Hispanics in the U.S.:
A Snapshot of the Year 2000

Why has the U.S. Latino consumer become such a prominent subject in financial and marketing circles? The answer is simple and straightforward: sheer business opportunity. For more than four decades, a significant number of emigrants from every country in Latin America have become active members of the U.S. consumer market. In less than forty years, the Hispanic market has more than quadrupled in size, a trend that is projected to continue for a long time. Between 1960 and 2000, the number of Hispanic consumers increased from 6.9 million to 31.4 million—11.4 percent of the total U.S. population—an absolute increase of 24.5 million people **(Figure 1.1)**.

The marketing challenge for companies wishing to sell to the Latino market is not only to identify Hispanics, but also to determine how they are

FIGURE 1.1

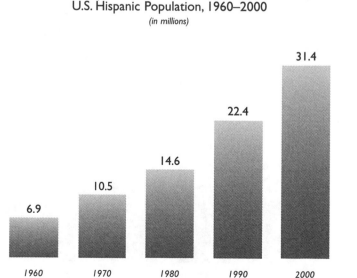

U.S. Hispanic Population, 1960–2000
(in millions)

Source: Cultural Access Group, based on U.S. Bureau of the Census

different from non-Hispanics and whether they are homogeneous as a group. Are Mexicans, Puerto Ricans, and Cubans alike? Is there a "Latino" culture that binds Hispanics together? What are Hispanics' likes and dislikes? How should businesses communicate with them? How should businesses factor into their marketing strategies the ongoing but slow acculturation process of Hispanics? Where can you find information about Hispanic consumers, and how can you reach them?

These and other considerations are explored in subsequent sections in Part I of *Marketing to American Latinos*. The present section provides a summary overview of the U.S. Hispanic market.

The statistics are impressive. The 21st century dawns with Hispanics in the United States estimated to exceed 31 million **(Figure 1.2)**, surpassing the population of Canada (30.2 million), and about 1.5 times the population of Australia (18.7 million). Between 1960 and 2000, the proportion of Hispanics in the United States

FIGURE 1.2

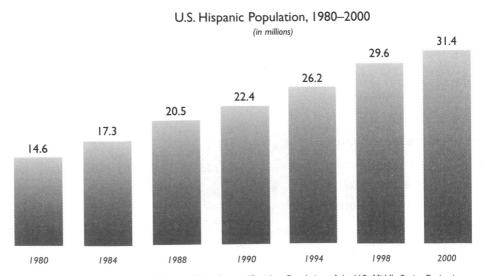

U.S. Hispanic Population, 1980–2000
(in millions)

1980	1984	1988	1990	1994	1998	2000
14.6	17.3	20.5	22.4	26.2	29.6	31.4

Source: Cultural Access Group, based on U.S. Bureau of the Census, "Resident Population of the U.S.: Middle Series Projections, 1996–2000," 1999; and Valdés, Scoane, 1995

tripled, from 3.9 percent to 11.4 percent **(Figure 1.3)**. In 1996 the nation's total foreign-born population was estimated at 25 million, of which more than 40 percent were Hispanics, giving the United States one of the largest Spanish-speaking populations in the world **(Figure 1.4)**.

FIGURE 1.3

Hispanic Population as Percentage of U.S. Population, 1960–2000

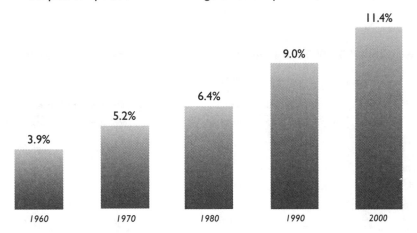

Source: Cultural Access Group, based on U.S. Bureau of the Census, "Resident Population of the U.S.: Middle Series Projections, 1996–2000," 1999

FIGURE 1.4

U.S. plus Four Latin American Countries with Large Spanish-Speaking Populations, 2000

The United States has one of the largest Spanish-speaking populations in the world.

Country	Population (Estimated)
Mexico	98,881,000
Colombia	42,321,000
Argentina	37,032,000
United States	**31,366,000**
Peru	25,662,000

Source: United Nations: Economic Commission for Latin America and the Caribbean (ECLAC); U.S. Census Bureau, "Resident Population of the U.S.: Middle Series Projections, 1996–2000," 1999

The number of households in 2000 is projected to double from the 1983 level, increasing from 4.7 million to more than 9.4 million. In absolute numbers, the U.S. Hispanic market added at least 2 million households between 1990 and 2000, a 31 percent increase. Black non-Hispanic households increased by 17 percent (1.7 million). White non–Hispanic households increased by 7.6 million or only 10 percent during the same decade **(Figures 1.5 and 1.6)**. The rapid growth of Hispanic households is expected to continue well into this century.

FIGURE 1.5

Household Growth, 1990–2000 and 1998–2003, by Race and Origin of Householder

(in thousands)

	Numerical Change		Percent Change	
	1990–2000	*1998–2003*	*1990–2000*	*1998–2003*
Total Households	13,373	5,452	14.5%	5.3%
White, non-Hispanics	7,601	2,488	10.3	3.1
Black, non-Hispanics	1,652	869	17.0	7.9
Asian and other, non-Hispanics*	963	517	39.2	16.1
Hispanic	**1,922**	**1,578**	**30.9**	**18.0**

* "Asian and other" from Exter, Regional Markets Vol. 2 / Households, 1999

Source: Updated from Exter, Regional Markets Vol. 2 / Households, 1999, based on Census Bureau data

FIGURE 1.6

Number of Households by Race and Origin of Householder, 1990–2003

(in thousands)

	1990	1998	2000	2003
Total Households	92,248	103,433	105,621	108,885
White, non-Hispanics	73,383	80,436	81,439	82,924
Black, non-Hispanics	9,733	11,041	11,386	11,910
Asian and other, non-Hispanics*	2,457	3,212	3,420	3,729
Hispanic	**6,220**	**8,744**	**9,376**	**10,322**

* "Asian and other" from Exter, Regional Markets Vol. 2 / Households, 1999

Source: Updated from Exter, Regional Markets Vol. 2 / Households, 1999, based on Census Bureau data

PURCHASING POWER

Hispanics in the continental United States are wealthier than most Hispanics living in Latin America. According to the University of Georgia, Selig Center of Economic Growth, U.S. Hispanic purchasing power increased dramatically during the 1990s, from $208 billion in 1990 to $383 billion in 1998, an 84.1 percent increase. However, despite a decline in the percentage of Hispanic households under the poverty level, the number of Hispanics living in poverty remained statistically unchanged at 15.8 million in 1998. According to the Census Bureau, in 1990 Latinos had a real per capita annual income of $9,204, which increased to $12,557 in 1999, a rise of 36.4 percent. This per capita income is higher than for any Latin American country **(Figure 1.7)**.

If current demographic and economic trends persist, the size of the U.S. Hispanic market and the amount of Hispanic disposable income will continue to grow significantly well into the 21st century.

From a business perspective, such unprecedented population and economic growth is reflected daily in the marketplace. A burgeoning number of Hispanic men, women, and children patronize supermarkets, automotive dealerships, general and specialty stores, and restaurants. They also conduct business in banks, credit unions, mortgage companies, and real estate and travel agencies.

These facts describing population, market size, and income growth show just a few trends in the Hispanic consumer market. To be effective, companies trying to sell to this market should learn more about the peculiarities of this rapidly growing population segment. They need to answer questions such as: what are Hispanics like collectively? How diverse is

FIGURE 1.7

Latino Income Growth

Hispanic income per capita is higher than in any Latin American county.

(1998 U.S. dollars)

	1990	1998
U.S. Hispanics	$9,204	$12,557*
Puerto Rico	6,470**	8,600
Venezuela	2,560	3,164
Uruguay	2,560	6,000
Mexico	2,490	4,360
Argentina	2,370	9,100
Chile	1,940	4,922
Costa Rica	1,910	2,900
El Salvador	1,100	1,980
Guatemala	900	1,455
Honduras	590	890

**1997 data   **1999 data*

Source: Cultural Access Group, based on U.S. Bureau of the Census, 1992b, 454; Population Reference Bureau, 1992; U.S. Department of State, Bureau of Inter-American Affairs, March 1998; Selig Center for Economic Growth, University of Georgia, "Hispanic Buying Power by Place of Residence 1990–1999," Nov-Dec. 1998

this population? How are Hispanic consumers different from general market consumers? What are their buying preferences? How can businesses effectively appeal to Hispanic consumers?

WHO IS HISPANIC?

Webster's Tenth New Collegiate Dictionary traces the origin of the word *Hispanic* to Spain's Hispania Iberian peninsula and defines as Hispanic any person "of Latin American descent living in the United States, especially one of Cuban, Mexican, or Puerto Rican origin." The Bureau of the Census used a more comprehensive definition at the time of the 1990 census. The bureau included as Hispanic persons in the categories Spanish, Spaniard, Mexican American, Chicano, Puerto Rican, Cuban, and "other" (to identify respondents from other parts of Latin America). Hispanic is also the preferred term used today within the business community to identify this particular segment of the market.

Many Mexican Americans tend to prefer the word Latino; Cubans appear to have no objection to the word Hispanic.

"LATINO" OR "HISPANIC"?

Often, the terms Latino and Hispanic are used interchangeably. Presently, Latino tends to be preferred by Hispanic consumers in some areas (e.g., California and Texas). When a particular Hispanic group is referred to, however, the name of the country of origin is usually used. In current usage, the term Latino refers more specifically to the peoples born in the Latin American region, regardless of race.

In sum, there is currently no consensus within the Hispanic community as to how to refer to its members collectively. The term Hispanic is neither offensive nor preferable. Latino Voices, a survey conducted among Mexicans, Puerto Ricans, and Cubans, found that foreign-born respondents overwhelmingly identified themselves with the name of their country of origin. The pattern of identification was similar among the U.S. native-born, particularly among Mexicans but to a lesser degree among Puerto Ricans and Cubans, who seemed to have a stronger preference for Pan-ethnic labels, such as Latino, Hispanic, or Spanish-American **(Figure 1.8)**.

FIGURE 1.8

Hispanic Self-Identification

*Foreign-born Mexicans, Puerto Ricans, and Cubans overwhelmingly
identified themselves with their country of origin.*

Place of Origin *(called themselves Mexican, Puerto Rican, Cuban)*

Pan-ethnic Names *(called themselves Hispanic, Latino, Spanish, Spanish American, Hispanic)*

American *(called themselves American)*

Other

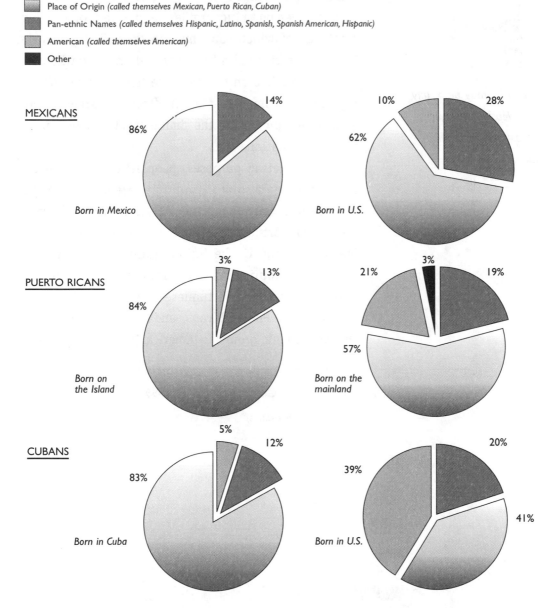

Note: People living in the U.S. were asked how they identified themselves. Numbers may not add up to 100 percent because of rounding.

Source: Cultural Access Group, reprinted from de la Garza, et al. *Latino Voiced: Mexican, Puertican and and Cuban Perspectives on American Politics*, Westview Press, 1992

Hispanics may be of any race. Most trace their ancestry to a Spanish-speaking country.

HISPANIC SUBGROUPS

As mentioned earlier, Hispanic is a convenient term used to address a large, heterogeneous group rich in diversity and cultural subtleties. Subgroups from each country have unique national histories, cultural backgrounds, demographic profiles, and levels of development—all of which contribute to their distinctiveness. Recognizing cultural differences and knowing when and how to capitalize on them or whether these can be disregarded is as important to an effective marketing program as learning to use the similarities that exist among the various nationalities.

For marketing purposes, people from Portugal and Brazil, who are also of Latin origin, are not included in the broad definition of the Hispanic market because they speak Portuguese. However, due to the increase in Brazilians living in the United States, as well as their presence as tourists, savvy corporations are targeting these consumers via Portuguese-language media.

Mexicans, Puerto Ricans, and Cubans are the three largest Hispanic groups in America **(Figure 1.9)**. People

FIGURE 1.9

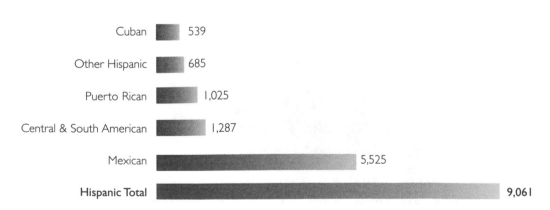

Hispanic Households by Country of Origin, 1999

(in thousands)

Cuban	539
Other Hispanic	685
Puerto Rican	1,025
Central & South American	1,287
Mexican	5,525
Hispanic Total	9,061

Source: Cultural Access Group, based on U.S. Bureau of the Census, Current Population Reports, February 2000

who trace their heritage to the countries of Central and South America form the other major Hispanic groups **(Figure 1.10)**. By virtue of being U.S. citizens, Puerto Ricans are in a separate category. Those who were born on the mainland and consider themselves Puerto Ricans are officially considered U.S. Hispanics. Those born on the U.S. Commonwealth island of Puerto Rico are counted separately, and are currently excluded from the United States Census Hispanic category. Because it would be erroneous to exclude Puerto Rico's population of 4 million from the figures for the U.S. Hispanic market, it is included where appropriate for analysis throughout this book.

From a marketing perspective, it makes a big difference whether consumers are born in the United States or in Latin America because foreign and native-born Hispanics differ considerably in terms of language usage, marketing maturity, media consumption, and cultural traits—all of which affect consumer research, marketing, and advertising strategies. The significance of the number of foreign-born Hispanics is hard to ignore. If

---

FIGURE 1.10

Cultural Diversity

U.S. Hispanic Population, 1999

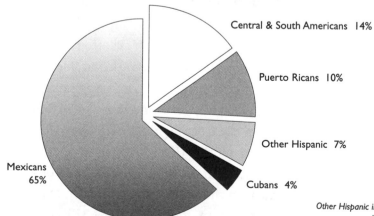

Central & South Americans 14%

Puerto Ricans 10%

Other Hispanic 7%

Cubans 4%

Mexicans 65%

Other Hispanic includes all other Hispanics or Latinos from regions not listed

Source: Cultural Access Group, from the U.S. Census Bureau, 2000

It is vital for marketers to take country of birth into account when targeting Hispanics, particularly Mexican, Central-American, and South-American consumers.

residents of Puerto Rico are added to the number of Hispanics living in the United States whose country of birth is other than the United States, the estimated total size of the Hispanic foreign-born market is 9 million, about 3 million more consumers than there are in the country of Switzerland.

It is vital for marketers to take country of birth into account when targeting Hispanics, particularly Mexican, Central-American, and South-American consumers. For these groups, which comprise a major share of the immigrant population, the proportion of foreign-born Americans has increased steadily in the past four decades and is projected to continue to do so for some time. Foreign-born Cubans outnumber the native-born population, despite a decline in immigration over the past decade.

Accordingly, it is also important to take into account that the number of foreign-born Americans is much higher than that given in the official count. As often publicized, a large number of legal and undocumented immigrants were not counted when the 1990 U.S. Census was taken.

GEOGRAPHIC DISTRIBUTION

To a large extent, the geographic location of the different Latin American countries relative to the United States has historically determined the settlement patterns of Hispanic immigrants. Puerto Ricans tend to relocate in the northeast (New York and Boston); Cubans in the southeast (Miami area); and Mexicans in the southwest (New Mexico, Texas, Arizona, and California).

Figure 1.11 details the distribution of the Hispanic population in the United States. Due to the shifting labor demands in growing service industries and industrial areas in the United States, Hispanics are relocating and migrating to "non-traditional" Hispanic cities. For example, Hispanic communities in Atlanta, Denver, Las

Vegas and other American cities are presently growing dramatically **(Figure 1.12)**.

Country of origin and relocation patterns of the immigrants have lent distinct characteristics to the rapidly growing Hispanic market.

FIGURE 1.11

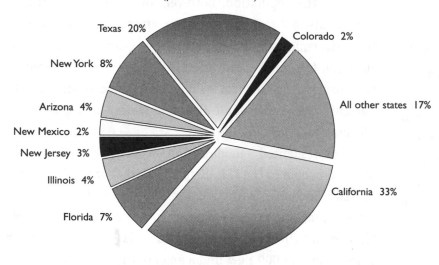

Hispanic Population for Selected States, 2000
(percent distribution)

Texas 20%
Colorado 2%
New York 8%
Arizona 4%
All other states 17%
New Mexico 2%
New Jersey 3%
Illinois 4%
California 33%
Florida 7%

Source: Cultural Access Group, based on Exter, Regional Markets Vol. 1 / Population, 1999, from Census Bureau data

FIGURE 1.12

Second Tier DMAs Ranked on Latino Population Growth 1990–2002

	DMA	Latino (%)	Non-Latino (%)
1	Las Vegas, NV	162.3	70.0
2	Ft. Smith, AR	142.4	27.1
3	Bend, OR	140.1	57.4
4	Atlanta, GA	110.3	33.0
5	Wilmington, NC	109.5	7.8
6	Omaha, NE	108.8	17.2
7	Knoxville, TN	108.2	15.2
8	Jonesboro, AR	106.6	10.2
9	Little Rock-Pine Bluff, AR	106.2	13.7
10	Minneapolis-St. Paul, MN	104.6	6.0

Source: Cultural Access Group, based on Claritas data, 1997

THE INVISIBLE HISPANIC MARKET

In addition to the 31.4 million U.S. resident Hispanics, there is a sizable uncounted Hispanic community, according to two different sources: the "undercount" of the U.S. Census and ongoing "undocumented" (or illegal) immigration. The official "undercount" for the total population of the U.S. is estimated at 3 percent. Undercounting has greater impact in specific segments of the population, however, and Hispanics, particularly immigrants, are more often undercounted. It is estimated that total Hispanics are undercounted by 6 percent (1.9 million). However, the undercount affects differently some segments of the Hispanic market, for example, Hispanic immigrants by 8 percent, and young adult Hispanic males, as a group, by 10 percent (Arce, NHCCI, 1997).

It is estimated that total Hispanics are undercounted by 6 percent (1.9 million), Hispanic immigrants by 8 percent, and young adult Hispanic males, as a group, by 10 percent.

Undocumented immigration contributes 160,000 to 180,000 people to the U.S. Hispanic market annually, a number partially included in the 31.4 million figure from the Census Bureau projections. According to Immigration and Naturalization Service (INS) data sources, Mexico is the source of slightly more than 150,000 new undocumented residents each year. It is presently estimated that there are about 2.7 million undocumented Mexicans. Many undocumented persons (about 41 percent) are "nonimmigrant overstays," that is, people who entered legally but never left **(Figure 1.13)**.

In marketing terms, this means that the 31.4 million Hispanic population underrepresents the purchase potential of the Hispanic market. In reality, the "continental" U.S. Hispanic market is closer to 34 million, adding the 1.9 million undercounted from the 1990 Census and assuming the "invisible" Hispanic market is growing at the same rate as the rest of the Hispanic market. With that adjustment, the U.S. Hispanic market may already be larger than the African American market.

Finally, if Puerto Rico's estimated 4 million people are added to the "continental" Hispanic market, the total U.S. Hispanic market stands at 38 million as we enter the new millennium.

FIGURE 1.13

Undocumented Immigrants from Latin America and other countries, October 1996

Country of Origin	Population	State of Residence	Population
All countries	5,000,000	All states	5,000,000
Hispanic Total	3,560,000	California	2,000,000
Mexico	2,700,000	Texas	700,000
El Salvador	335,000	New York	540,000
Guatemala	165,000	Florida	350,000
Honduras	90,000	Illinois	290,000
Nicaragua	70,000	New Jersey	135,000
Colombia	65,000	Arizona	115,000
Ecuador	55,000	Massachusetts	85,000
Dominican Republic	50,000	Virginia	55,000
Peru	30,000	Washington	52,000
		Colorado	45,000
Non-Hispanic Total	1,440,000	Maryland	44,000
Canada	120,000	Michigan	37,000
Haiti	105,000	Pennsylvania	37,000
Philippines	95,000	New Mexico	37,000
Poland	70,000	Oregon	33,000
Bahamas	70,000	Georgia	32,000
Trinidad & Tobago	50,000	District of Columbia	30,000
Jamaica	50,000	Connecticut	29,000
Pakistan	41,000	Other	330,000
Nevada	24,000		
India	33,000		
Dominica	32,000		
Korea	30,000		
Other	744,000		

Source: Cultural Access Group, based on Statistics: Illegal Alien Resident Population, Immigration and Naturalization Service, INS, 1996

Chapter 2

Hispanic Past and Present

Most foreign-born Latino immigrants do not speak fluent English during their first ten to fifteen years of residence in the United States.

Hispanic presence in what is now the United States dates back to 1513. The number of Hispanic immigrants swelled after World War II. Many were "imported" by regional state governments to provide a labor force during the war. That is, for example, the main reason for migration of Mexicans to Chicago by 1945. Many Mexican families settled in what became the United States long before Texas and California were incorporated into the Union. Recent surveys identify various motives for relocating to the United States. Of these, economic considerations rate highest among Mexicans, whereas avoidance of political strife dominates among Cuban immigrants (de la Garza et al., 1992). Family reunification, educational opportunities, new sources of financial investment, and the desire to start a new business in the United States are also important contributors to Hispanic immigration **(Figure 2.1)**. Presently, the United States is experiencing a major industrial explosion, which demands labor in many industries and serves as a beacon for immigration. For example, the semiconductor industry in California, Texas, Colorado, New Mexico, New York, and New Jersey, with its growing need for professional, technical, and semiskilled labor, is a major beneficiary of the presence of Hispanics in the United States.

FIGURE 2.1

Hispanic Immigrants' Reasons for Coming to the U.S.

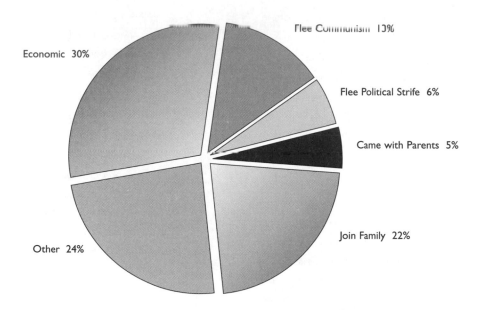

Flee Communism 13%

Economic 30%

Flee Political Strife 6%

Came with Parents 5%

Join Family 22%

Other 24%

Source: Cultural Access Group, based on NALEO Educational Fund. Cited in Schick and Schick, 1991

Figure 2.2 lists important sociopolitical landmarks in the history of the United States, Puerto Rico, Mexico, Cuba, and Central and South America that are at the core of the massive migration of Hispanics to the United States. From the early years until today, they and their descendants have been active members of American society.

To understand today's Hispanic market, marketers need to realize that Hispanic consumers come from many different countries and many different backgrounds. Men, women, and children come from urban and rural areas, from all over North, Central, and South America and from the Caribbean. Some have more formal schooling than others. Many families arrived during the

Continues on page 20

FIGURE 2.2

Chronology of Hispanic Presence in the United States

SPANISH

1690	First permanent Spanish settlement in Texas.
1691	Expansion to Arizona and Texas.
1766	San Francisco presidio becomes the northernmost frontier Spanish outpost.
1769	First Spanish mission in Alta, California (San Diego).

MEXICAN

1781	Independence from New Spain. The Republic of Mexico is born.
1821	Mexico acquires its independence from Spain. Permanent colonies exist in coastal California, southern Arizona, southern Texas, southern Colorado, and most of Texas.
1822	Anglo colonization of Mexican Texas begins at the request of Mexican representatives.
1836	Anglo settlers declare the Republic of Texas independent of Mexico. Mexicans are forced off their properties and many move to Mexico.
1845	Texas is officially annexed to the United States.
1846	The United States invades Mexico. The treaty of Guadalupe ends the war. Half of land area of Mexico (including Texas, California, most of Arizona and New Mexico, parts of Colorado, Utah and Nevada) is ceded to the United States. About 75,000 people choose to become U.S. citizens.
1880	Mexican immigration to the United States is stimulated by the advent of the railroad.
1910	Mexican revolution begins. Hundreds of people flee from Mexico and settle in the southwestern United States.
1917	During World War I, "temporary" Mexican farm workers, railroad laborers, and miners are permitted to enter the United States to work.
1917	Immigration Act, imposing literacy requirement on all immigrants, is designed to curtail immigration from Asia and Eastern Europe. Mexico and Puerto Rico become major sources of workers.

CUBAN

1563	Earliest settlement in North America in Saint Augustine, Florida.
1770-90	50,000 African slaves are reportedly taken to Cuba to work in sugar production.
1776	Spanish presence expands in Florida, which is ceded by the French.
1783	The United States purchases Florida from Spain.
1840-70	125,000 Chinese arrive in Cuba to work as cane-cutters, build railroads, and serve as domestics in the cities. Retail trade expands with the influx of Spaniard merchants, who open the first general stores, called *bodegas*.
1868	Cubans leave for Europe and the United States in sizable numbers during Cuba's first major attempt at independence.

1880   Slavery is abolished. Population becomes more heterogeneous.

1897   Spain grants autonomy to Cuba and Puerto Rico.

1898   Treaty of Paris between Spain and the United States grants Cuba and Puerto Rico to the United States.

1902   Cuba declares its independence from the United States.

1959   Castro takes power. Large-scale immigration to the United States.

1965   Second wave of Cuban refugees includes many relatives of former exiles.

1966-73   Cuban airlift. About 10 percent of the island population emigrates during this time. Most are of European origin, middle-class, well educated, landowners, professionals, and business people.

1980   Third wave of Cuban refugees, *Marielitos*, who are less educated, are of lower economic status, and are mostly non-European, begins to immigrate to the United States.

1994   *Balceros*, or rafters, flee harsh economic conditions in Cuba. Thousands arrive in the United States; many are picked up at sea by U.S. Coast Guard and are taken back to the U.S. base at Guantanamo, Cuba, where temporary camps are set up.

PUERTO RICAN

1898   In the Treaty of Paris, Spain transfers Puerto Rico and Cuba to the United States.

1900   The Foraker Act establishes a civilian government in Puerto Rico under U.S. dominance. Islanders elect their own House of Representatives but are not allowed to vote in Washington.

1930   United States controls 44 percent of cultivated land in Puerto Rico. Private capital controls 60 percent of banks, public services and all maritime lines.

1930-34   About 20 percent of Puerto Ricans on the mainland return to the island.

1944   Operation Bootstrap is initiated by the Puerto Rican government to meet U.S. labor demands of World War II. Encourages industrialization in the island and stimulates migration to the mainland.

1950   Puerto Rico becomes a U.S. commonwealth.

1950-60   Early employment pattern: menial jobs in service sector, light factory work.

1959   Unlike Mexicans or Cubans, Puerto Ricans encounter minimum red tape to enter or re-enter the United States.

1978   The United Nations recognizes Puerto Rico as a colony of the United States.

Source: Kanellos, *The Hispanic American Almanac,* 1993

past twenty years; others have resided in the United States for many generations. Large numbers come alone, others with their families.

Most foreign-born Latino immigrants do not speak fluent English during their first ten to fifteen years of residence in the United States. Despite their diversity, their cultural similarities, such as the Spanish language and cultural traits, far outweigh their differences.

HISPANIC HERITAGE AND CULTURAL NETWORKS

Unlike the period preceding World War II, the past four decades have witnessed an influx of Hispanic immigrants into the United States from Puerto Rico, Cuba, Mexico, the Dominican Republic, and Central and South America. Net migration gains combined with more births than deaths, and political, economic, and social factors have greatly enhanced the visibility of Hispanics throughout the United States.

Today Hispanics are well established in American society. They have developed a social infrastructure through which the ideas and values of their culture are preserved and transmitted to future generations. Hispanics' rapid population growth, purchasing power, business entrepreneurship, expanding communities, political participation, and communication networks, along with the growth of organizations dedicated to the study and preservation of Hispanic history and culture, have created a distinct Hispanic niche in the American marketplace and society.

HISPANIC ENTREPRENEURS

Not only are Hispanics significant consumers of mass market U.S. goods, they also contribute greatly to the marketplace as entrepreneurs and producers of goods and services, and as employers. In 1992 there were 862,605 Hispanic-owned businesses in the United States, up from 422,373 in 1987, with total sales and receipts tripling to $76.8 billion from $25 billion **(Figure 2.3)**. More recently, 1997 *Hispanic Business* magazine projections, based on Census Bureau data, show the "Golden Trio" states—California, Texas and Florida—with 456,000, 248,000, and 222,000 registered Hispanic businesses, respectively.

California is responsible for the lion's share—25 per-cent—of all sales receipts generated nationwide by Hispanic-owned businesses. Revenues were projected to reach $42 billion in 1997. Florida follows with $39 billion, and Texas with $21 billion (**Figure 2.4**). The lat-est U.S. Census data on Hispanic-owned businesses, 1992, shows that Hispanic entrepreneurship is strong

FIGURE 2.3

Growth of Hispanic-Owned Firms, Revenues, and Employees

Survey Year	Number of Businesses	Annual Growth (*percent*)	Revenue (*in billions*)	Percentage Annual Growth	Number of Employees	Annual Growth (*percent*)
1969	100,212	—	$3.6	—	126,296	—
1972	120,108	6	5.3	14	149,656	6
1977	219,355	13	10.4	14	206,054	7
1982	233,975	1	11.8	2	154,791	6
1987	422,373	13	24.7	16	264,846	11
1992*	862,605	15	76.8	25	—	—

Online Release, 1992

Notes: Growth percentages are expressed as compound annual rates. Data for surveys before 1982 reflect some differences from current methodology. However, the apparent slow growth between 1977 and 1982, including the decrease in employment, is real and reflects general economic conditions.

Source: Cultural Access Group, based on U.S. Bureau of the Census, August 1990–June 1991; 1980

FIGURE 2.4

Three States with Largest Number of Hispanic-Owned Businesses

1997 Projections

State	Hispanic Firms	Revenues (*in thousands*)	Employees
California	455,663	$ 42,092,700	315,383
Texas	248,160	$ 21,860,109	238,846
Florida	221,995	$ 39,002,497	281,160

Source: Cultural Access Group, based on 1997 projections by *Hispanic Business*; U.S. Census data

across the nation **(Figure 2.5)**. This creates opportunities for business-to-business marketing. The financial and insurance industries have already targeted this growing business sector, but other industries such as high-technology—computer companies, Internet providers, software companies, and related office equipment—have been slow to take advantage of this marketing and sales opportunity. The "new" Hispanic marketing boom coupled with the U.S. Census 2000 data should help these companies discover this pot of gold.

FIGURE 2.5

Ten States with the Largest Hispanic Businesses Ranked by States, 1992

State	Firms (number)	Sales and Receipts (in thousands)	Paid Employees (number)
California	249,717	$19,552,637	182,205
Texas	155,909	11,796,301	138,798
Florida	118,208	16,127,202	125,935
New York	50,601	4,732,279	34,825
New Jersey	22,198	2,827,937	21,803
New Mexico	21,586	1,479,650	19,004
Illinois	18,368	1,950,685	17,499
Arizona	17,835	1,298,084	16,559
Colorado	13,817	1,212,137	13,139
Virginia	7,654	957,962	5,966
Total	675,893	61,934,874	575,733

Number of employees may be lower than number of firms because only paid employees are included, not owners or unpaid family members who work in the firm.

Source: Cultural Access Group, based on U.S. Census, Statistics for Hispanic-Owned Firms by State: 1992

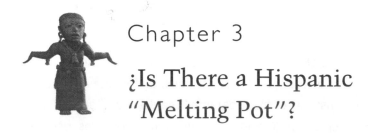

Chapter 3

¿Is There a Hispanic "Melting Pot"?

Abundant research conducted over the past two decades makes clear that important and identifiable cultural traits can be found in U.S. Hispanic families even when they have resided in the United States for several generations. In other words, the "melting pot" phenomenon is slow to occur, and much slower than some had predicted.

Of all social traits, language is perhaps the most distinguishable characteristic of any culture and probably the last one any immigrant group will relinquish. As has been documented extensively, given the choice, most foreign-born and many first-generation U.S. Hispanic adults speak in Spanish rather than English, even if they are bilingual.

Spanish-language usage will continue well into the future if current immigration projections hold. According to Edmonston and Passel (1992), by the year 2010, foreign-born Hispanic consumers may still account for about 40 percent (13.6 million) of the total Hispanic market, and second and later generations for about 60 percent (20.4 million).

"MULTICULTURAL" HOUSEHOLDS

"Multicultural" households are common in the U.S. Hispanic marketplace. Presently, few adult Hispanic consumers have acquired their values and behaviors from mainstream American culture. Rather, their aspirations, lifestyles, preferences and purchasing behavior tend to be different from those of the non-Hispanic market. In the Hispanic marketplace, foreign-born or first-generation consumers have preferences and tastes that were acquired and molded in their countries of origin. In contrast, Hispanic children and teens raised in the United States usually acquire some of their values and preferences from their exposure to American culture through schools, friends, and media as well as from the beliefs and customs of their parents. The daily contact of Hispanic children with both Anglo and Hispanic traditions gives rise to households with different value systems and dual preferences for clothing, foods, and other consumer goods. For these reasons, even within the household, Hispanic families can frequently exhibit distinct sets of aspirations, behaviors, food preferences, cooking styles, consumption habits, and so on.

CULTURAL AND REGIONAL DIFFERENCES

During the Age of Discovery (circa 1500), Spain, and to a lesser extent Portugal, conquered large regions of the Western Hemisphere, including most of Central America, South America, the Caribbean, Mexico, and parts of what is today the United States, specifically, Texas, Arizona, and California. Hence, the most common cultural features shared by nearly all Latin American countries are the Spanish language and the Catholic faith.

Other factors connect Latin American countries with Spain and Portugal as well. They include slower economic, technological, and scientific development (Spain and Portugal were two of the last countries to join the Industrial Revolution). Partly because of this slower development, many Latin American countries still have large rural or semirural populations with little formal education. Most of these countries are not well developed, and they all share in the struggle to compete with more technologically and economically advanced nations, spawning a greater impetus for immigration for those in search of technological advantage, otherwise referred to as the "brain drain."

In addition, most Latin American countries were also greatly influenced by indigenous cultures, having had their own pre-Columbian civilizations, such as, the Mayan and Aztec in Mexico and the Incan in Peru. Others, such as Argentina, Uruguay, Chile, Peru, Paraguay, Cuba, and the Dominican Republic, were also influenced by large immigration flows from northern and eastern Europe, Africa, and Asia during the 19th and 20th centuries. The influence of these various cultures is pervasive in the music Latinos enjoy singing and dancing to, as well as the different foods they eat, the religious and healing practices they follow, and their material goods, such as musical instruments and artifacts.

Cultural and regional differences become very relevant when the target audience is a particular Hispanic subgroup.

ACCULTURATION IN AMERICA

As with immigrants from other cultures, upon arrival in the United States, today's Hispanic immigrants come into contact with a different culture. Almost immediately, they begin to realize that the lifestyles, customs, aspirations, and values found in the new society are different from their own. What they considered a given in their own country is now questioned, reassessed, and sometimes replaced with a different viewpoint, lifestyle or way of doing things. As they become familiar with the traditions and the way of life in the United States, Hispanics develop new approaches to interacting, living, and understanding the world around them. Slowly but steadily, the acculturation process begins and carries on.

Gradually, Hispanic consumers start to shift from their native culture to that of the United States. Not everyone acculturates at the same pace. Many factors may accelerate or slow the process, such as personality of the individual, where immigrants relocate, or the degree of formal education they have upon arrival. The process of acculturation takes place at all levels of social interaction. Understanding its dynamics is critical to learning how to interact, communicate, and work with the Hispanic consumer market successfully.

Because new immigrants arrive daily, the Hispanic market acculturation process is continuously evolving, fueled in part by Hispanic culture coming of age with a strong presence in the music and entertainment culture. For example, Ricky Martin's extraordinary popularity across all population segments, along with that of Gloria Estefan, Jennifer Lopez and many others, is evidence of this dynamic. Advertisers

To be effective, campaigns targeting Hispanic consumers must be in consonance with Hispanic culture at all message levels: symbolic, explicit, visual and subliminal.

and others who continually communicate with Hispanic customers and consumers need to do so at all levels of the cultural assimilation process. Ad campaigns and other marketing efforts targeting Hispanics must successfully communicate with a market that is conspicuously new, as well as one that is well informed, brand aware, and loyal. Acculturation as it relates to the Hispanic consumer market is a complex yet manageable process that is addressed in-depth later in this book.

Communication is a critical aspect during the transition between cultures. When two or more cultures coexist in the same society, as is the case with Anglo and Hispanic cultures, there is a greater risk that the receiver belonging to a culture different from the sender's will misinterpret the intended meaning in the message being delivered, even when the translated words are correct. The result is miscommunication and wasted dollars. To be effective, campaigns targeting Hispanic consumers must be in consonance with Hispanic culture at all message levels: symbolic, explicit, visual and subliminal.

MANAGING LANGUAGE COMPLEXITY

"Pardon Me, Do You Speak English?" (Crispell, 1992) is the title of an article reporting data on a growing American phenomenon of "linguistically isolated households," the term the U.S. Census uses for households in which no one is able to speak English well enough to communicate with English-speaking people. These households are also isolated from American culture. Their members are excluded from mainstream American culture and, to a large extent, unreachable via traditional English-language marketing and advertising strategies.

Most community-based vendors talk to their customers in Spanish. Catholic churches, representing the dominant religion for Hispanics, reach their congregations through services conducted in Spanish. Shops and supermarkets satisfy consumers' longing for traditional Hispanic foods, clothing, and amenities along with their newly acquired tastes for American products. Given the share of immigration from Latin America to the United States **(Figure 3.1)**, and immigration projections beyond the year 2000, Spanish will continue to be a popular language in the United States and will certainly be an effective tool for marketing to Hispanics—adults in particular—in the foreseeable future.

Spanish will continue to be a popular language in the United States and an effective tool for marketing to Hispanics.

SPANISH PREFERENCE

Many consumer studies indicate that adult consumers' preference for the Spanish language is perhaps the strongest indicator of Hispanic culture in the United States. After conducting thousands of interviews among Hispanic adults, Cultural Access Group developed the

FIGURE 3.1

Legal Immigration by Country of Origin, 1997–1994

	1997	1996	1995	1994	Total	Percent
All	798,378	915,900	720,461	804,416	3,239,155	100.0%
Mexico	146,865	163,572	89,932	111,398	511,767	15.8
Central America	43,676	44,289	31,814	39,908	159,687	4.9
Caribbean	105,299	116,801	96,788	104,804	423,692	13.1
South America	52,877	61,769	45,666	47,377	207,689	6.4
Total Hispanic	348,717	386,431	264,200	303,487	1,302,835	40.2
Asia	265,786	307,807	267,931	292,589	1,134,113	35.0
Europe	119,898	147,581	128,185	160,916	556,580	17.2
All Other	63,977	74,081	60,145	47,424	245,627	7.6

Source: Cultural Access Group, NuStats, (1999) from INS Reports, Paper presented at the National Hispanic Corporate Council Institute, (NHCCI) Advanced Seminar, Denver, August, 1999

Age and length of residence in the U.S. helps determine language of preference.

Hispanic Language Segmentation©, a rating scale based on a battery of questions concerning usage and proficiency in Spanish and English. On that basis, in conjunction with respondents' language preference in media, Cultural Access Group identified five groups in the Hispanic market today:

- Spanish Only
- Spanish Preferred
- True Bilinguals
- English Preferred
- English Only

Language segmentation simplifies the challenge of targeting Hispanic consumer segments successfully in-language and in-culture.

VARIATIONS IN MEDIA USAGE

Most Hispanics use both English and Spanish media. The frequency with which they choose one or the other, however, varies drastically depending on age, language proficiency, length of residence in the United States and formal educational level. As would be expected, the fewer the number of years that Hispanic adults have lived in the United States, the lower their English proficiency and the greater the use of Spanish-language media. This rule, however, does not apply across the board. Many long-term U.S. residents, and even second-generation Hispanics, choose more Spanish-language media than English-language media. Conversely, some young adults and teens prefer English-language media, consistent with their age and lifestyles, even if they have resided in the United States for only a few years.

As would be expected, Hispanic, English-Only, and English-Preferred segments partake of significantly more English than Spanish-language media, but it must be kept in mind that they are still a small percentage of the total U.S. Hispanic market. Since a large proportion of Hispanics arrived in the United States during the 1980s and 1990s, the Spanish-Only and Spanish-Preferred segments of the market are significant, particularly among adults.

It stands to reason that Spanish should be the language selected to advertise to adults such products as home improvement, food, insurance and other financial products, travel, entertainment, cars, restaurants, over-the-counter medicines, and health-care services. English-language media play the same informational role to True-Bilinguals and English-Preferred consumers as to the general market. Therefore, Spanish- and English-language media complement each other in Hispanic marketing communication strategies. However, our research has shown that acculturated Hispanics tend to respond more to "in-culture" advertising that is culturally attuned, even if the message itself is delivered in English.

A "HOME AWAY FROM HOME"

Regardless of how long Hispanic consumers have lived in the United States, foreign-born Hispanics all had to leave their homes, their families, their friends, and the way they used to live. Some fled economic strife, others escaped political persecution, and still others had to face deportation.

Whatever the reasons, many Hispanics think of their native countries with longing and nostalgia, and dream of going back home someday, while others have happily embraced their new home country. Cubans in particular know they will never return. A need to create a home away from home has resulted in the development of small Latin corners. For example, Miami is known as Little Havana, and Southern California is "a piece of Latin America." Regardless of their country of origin,

Currently, Hispanics in the Los Angeles basin account for more than 45 percent of the total population of the area.

the immigration experience contributes to the character and strength of U.S. Hispanics. They are nostalgic, courageous, hardworking, and committed to contributing to the growth of their new homeland.

Most Hispanic *barrios*, or neighborhoods, have evolved into well-organized communities with their own city council representatives, community activists, school boards, medical clinics, legal offices, and nonprofit organizations. One of the most important social functions these communities provide is a sense of belonging—of cultural heritage.

Hispanics have become active in the United States political process and are influential at the federal, state, county, city and local levels. In 1999 there were 4,965 elected Hispanic officials including 51 state senators, 18 federal representatives and 135 state representatives **(Figure 3.2)**.

FIGURE 3.2

Hispanics in Government

In 1999, nearly 5,000 Hispanics held elected office in the U.S.

Senators	0
U.S. Representatives	18
State Level	
State Senators	51
State Executives	9
State Representatives	135
Local Level	
County Officials	376
Municipal Officials	1,343
Judicial / Law Enforcement	492
Educational / School Board Members	2,414
Special District Officials	127
TOTAL	**4,965**

Source: NALEO Educational Fund's 1999 National Directory of Latino Elected Officials, Los Angeles, CA

Further, Hispanics may soon be the majority population in states such as New Mexico, California, and Texas. In 2000, Hispanics comprised an estimated 45, 35, and 33 percent, respectively, of the total population of those states **(Figures 3.3, 3.4,** and **3.5)**. Currently, Hispanics in the Los Angeles basin account for more than 45 percent of the total population of the area.

In their home countries, most immigrant Hispanics encountered the hardship of having to earn a living in a society where social and

FIGURE 3.3

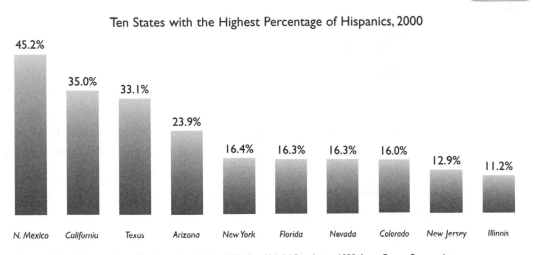

Ten States with the Highest Percentage of Hispanics, 2000

Source: Cultural Access Group, based on Exter, Regional Markets Vol. 1 / Population, 1999, from Census Bureau data

FIGURE 3.4

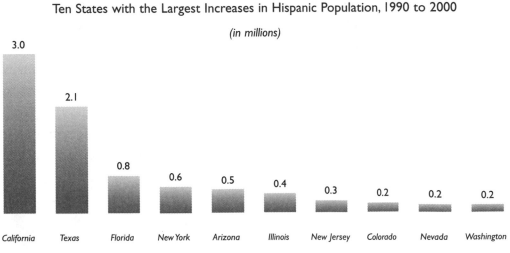

Ten States with the Largest Increases in Hispanic Population, 1990 to 2000

(in millions)

Source: Cultural Access Group, based on Exter, Regional Markets Vol. 1 / Population, 1999, from Census Bureau data

FIGURE 3.5

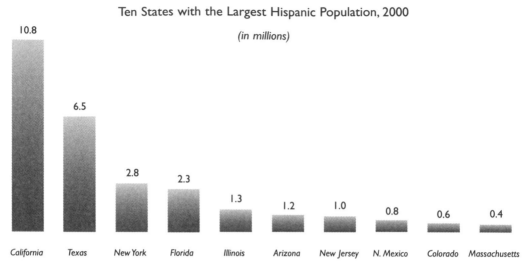

Ten States with the Largest Hispanic Population, 2000

(in millions)

Source: Data from Exter, Regional Markets Vol. 1 / Population, 1999, based on Census Bureau data

political conditions are so oppressive that it is often difficult to achieve acceptable or minimal social status or material gains. One of the greatest attributes Hispanics see in the United States is its political freedom and the opportunities available for upward mobility, brought about by an open and democratic society. The simple fact that such a large group of people attempts to move between countries in order to improve their living conditions reveals their eagerness to climb the socioeconomic ladder, and their determination to work hard and succeed for the sake of their children's future.

Regardless of the reasons for leaving their home countries, Hispanics arrive in the United States searching for a better life and a higher standard of living. Although as a group Hispanics may be at a disadvantage relative to other immigrants with regard to formal education, income, and work experience, they have certainly advanced their status. Their social, economic, and political gains during the past few decades exemplify their potential to be active contributors to American society and the marketplace. It is expected that Hispanics will continue to make gains and contributions at all levels in society.

SECTION 2

IN-CULTURE
ADVERTISING

Chapter 4

The "In-Culture" Difference

In 1987, Cultural Access Group Access Worldwide (formerly Hispanic Market Connections, Inc.), a marketing research company, adopted the slogan, "It's not only a matter of language." At the time, advertising to Hispanic consumers via Spanish-language media had already been established. It made good business sense. Companies like Kraft, Procter & Gamble, General Foods, Colgate, and Coca-Cola had been doing it for years with enormous success. So why the slogan?

Advertisers were certainly on the right track in their strategy to use the Spanish language, but in many cases when the Hispanic market strategy was, for example, a direct translation of the general market strategy, something was missing. The Spanish-language messages directed to consumers lacked "cultural attunement," with which Hispanic people could identify. It was akin to showing non-Asians eating their meals with chopsticks. As a consequence, the Spanish-language campaigns were not reaching as many consumers and were not as effective as they could be. The Spanish-language syntax used was correct, but the images, symbols and experiences were wrong. Hispanic-consumer market research showed that the use of Spanish language was essential to reach this growing share of the U.S. market, but language alone was not the only key to gaining Hispanic customers. These marketing campaigns were not in-culture.

Different cultures have distinct ways of perceiving, organizing, relating to and interacting with society.

COMMUNICATING "IN-CULTURE"

Different cultures have distinct ways of perceiving, organizing, relating to and interacting with society. What is perfectly acceptable in one culture may not be acceptable in another. To have an impact, the message needs to fit the cultural context and the mind-set of the audience being targeted. Imagine, for instance, a situation in which people from the same part of the world converse with dear friends. They all speak the same language at many levels. In all societies, language is a common cultural bond, but it is only one element among many. There are many other things, including events, customs, friends, dress codes, salutations, and inexplicit protocols that may be typical of one group and not another. The attitudes, behaviors and values vary among cultures so what makes sense (or is "in consonance") to members of one group may mystify others. All these elements are present implicitly in dialogue, and we tend to take it for granted that they are the same across cultures, but they may not be.

For example, in many European countries it is acceptable for males to greet each other with a kiss, whereas this would be unacceptable for most Americans. This behavioral difference in greeting protocol is the result of the meaning of the kiss in each society. In some European cultures, the greeting kiss between males means deep, dear affection, whereas in the United States it has an erotic connotation. This simple example illustrates the relevance of learning to "manage" culture as well as language differences. In sum, to communicate successfully with consumers from another culture, it is necessary to do more than just speak the language; one must speak the culture.

In addition, the longer foreign-born Hispanics reside in the United States, the greater their exposure to U.S. culture, and hence, the greater the chance that they acquire at least some American cultural values and traits. This process of cultural adaptation is referred to as acculturation, and is discussed in more detail later in this section.

In today's business environment, most business managers and marketing executives know they need to have the Hispanic consumer's perspective and insight in order to get successful results from their marketing and advertising campaigns. They know they cannot draw directly from personal experience or look at general market strategies or rules of thumb to make the necessary Hispanic marketing decisions.

This section addresses culture, cultural issues, and the acculturation process. It also describes tools for managing the acculturation process and diversity within the Hispanic market.

WHAT IS CULTURE?

There are more than 100 definitions of culture and explanations of what culture means. Yet, it can be almost universally agreed that culture is at the core of an individual's behavior and has a profound effect on the individual's degree of assimilation. For the purpose of discussing Hispanics, acculturation and marketing, a broad definition is in order.

Culture, in broad terms, may be defined as "the system of social institutions, traditions, values, and beliefs that characterize a particular social group or country and which are systematically transmitted to succeeding generations" (adapted from Hamburg, 1975). In other words, culture describes life strategy in all its various components—aspirations; dreams; and emotional, physical, and metaphysical behavioral traits (McGuill, 1983) Culture encompasses everything a person has seen and heard from birth—from parents, grandparents, siblings, friends, schoolteachers, radio and TV programs, the clergy, etc. It is the repository of knowledge, experiences, beliefs, meanings, notions of time, spatial relations, concepts of the universe and other elements acquired in the course of generations through individuals, groups and mass media.

To have an impact, a marketing message needs to fit the cultural context and mind-set of the audience being targeted.

HOW THE BRAIN WORKS

Our culture then determines how we are programmed to experience life. This invisible program sets up our beliefs and values, and a chain reaction begins, according to Fons Trompenaars in his book, *Riding the Waves of Culture.*

1. Programming creates beliefs

2. Beliefs create attitudes

3. Attitudes create feelings

4. Feelings determine actions

5. Actions create results.

Societies give status to people based on different "programs." Some accord status to a person on the basis of what he or she does for a living or on personal achievement. Others ascribe status based on social class, gender, education or religious background. In his book mentioned above, Dr. Trompenaars, who has conducted extensive research on cross-culture marketing presents a wealth of data and examples as to how different cultures see the world and how they relate to each other. He also discusses how gaining basic insights into the different cultural "programs" can help determine whether an advertising campaign is successful.

For example, Latinos tend to be highly status driven. They ascribe status based on "who you are" (ascription). In comparison, Anglo-Saxons tend to ascribe status on the basis of "what you do" (achievement). Hence, recognizing this core difference can help managers position or present their product or service from a perspective that reflects these differences. An Anglo-Saxon message could say, "This is good for you," whereas the Latino message would say, "This is good for the family."

DEALING WITH CULTURAL DIFFERENCES

The cultural divide between Hispanics and other Americans is still wide. A significant number of Hispanic men and women arrive in the United States as adults, bringing with them the experiences, lifestyles, expectations, values, legends and dreams acquired in their Latino, non-Anglo-Saxon societies. A survey found that "almost two-thirds of Mexicans and 80 percent of Cubans [interviewed] emigrated to the U.S. as adults" (de la Garza, 1992). The extent to which these immigrants participate in American society affects how fast they learn the American ways of life, as well as their interpretation and perception of advertising messages and images.

As previously mentioned, lack of "cultural affinity" can diminish the effectiveness of an advertising message. Certain products, brands, services and their use may be common knowledge to the general market, but this does not mean that foreign-born or newly arrived Hispanic consumers have the same knowledge.

For example, studies by the Cultural Access Group have shown how Hispanic consumers experience differs with various products and services. One study showed that some Hispanics in the west and southwest prefer to wash their hair with soap rather than shampoo because it is the way they used to do it "back home" and "it works." Yet, in other areas, like Miami and New York, this behavior did not exist among Hispanic women. Another study on infant care revealed that some Hispanic women continue to wrap their newborn babies tightly with a cloth to "make sure the belly button heals safely;" others do not bathe their infants until their belly button has healed.

As an example, studies show that depending on the country of origin, or the degree of urbanization of their

Almost two-thirds of Mexicans and 80 percent of Cubans [interviewed] emigrated to the U.S. as adults.

former place of residence, recent immigrants may not know about new developments in the telecommunications industry and hence, see no difference between purchasing a rotary phone or a digital phone. So, when telephone companies want to market "call forwarding" or "three-way calling" services to Hispanic customers, they need to market not only the service, but the whole concept of digital phone service.

These are but a few examples illustrating how Hispanic consumers from different countries can relate to or use a product differently, and the importance of cultural affinity in marketing communications. Messages, creative strategies, visuals, and symbols must be selected with the consumer's sociocultural background in mind. The point is not that marketers and advertisers promote those old behavior practices (e.g., not bathing an infant), but that they be aware that the cultural differences exist, and then decide on an appropriate strategy—one that will have an impact on the behavior, one specific to the consumer's native culture.

In addition, to successfully communicate with Hispanic consumers, marketers need to be aware of and learn how to connect with dominant Hispanic cultural traits, such as the importance of family, their attitudes toward children, the traditional roles of men and women, the "new" Latina culture, and how these cultural traits vary with bilingual, bicultural consumers.

CULTURAL VS. SOCIOECONOMIC DIFFERENCES

Culture is an abstract concept or a hypothetical construct that may be too broad and oversimplified when applied to an entire group of people, as it is to "Hispanics" in this book. It is usually true that a greater difference is found when the various socioeconomic classes are compared than when ethnic groups are compared within each class. It has been suggested to this author that many working-class Americans are more closely aligned with the Hispanic value orientation than that of middle-class Americans **(Figure 4.1)**. Similarly, international research findings show that the "average U.S. Hispanic" culture is closer to the working-class culture in countries where Spanish or a Latin-based language is spoken (e.g., Central and South America, Mexico, Spain, Italy, France, and Portugal) than to that of the middle or upper class of these societies. Again, this suggests that some of the cultural differences observed may be more socioeconomic than ethnic in nature. In other words, for purposes of discussing differences between the two groups, "Hispanic" and "Anglo" are used as catch-alls to refer to the "average" or most common value orientation of each ethnic group in the U.S.

Broader cultural differences reflecting the traits of the "average U.S. Hispanic" and the "average, middle-class American" are listed in **Figure 4.2**.

FIGURE 4.1

Value Orientation Differences Between Hispanics and the American Middle Class

	Hispanics	Anglos
How we see and define ourselves	As part of a family clan or group	Within ourselves, as individuals
Whom we rely on for help	Family, friends, community (Hispanic "social security")	Ourselves and institutions
What we value in people	Stress differences, show respect	Minimize differences, everybody's the same
What we stress in relationships	Respect, cooperation, formality	Symmetrical interpersonal relationships, informality, competition
Children	Dependence, obedience	Independence, egalitarian
Family	Defined roles, hierarchy, old men know more than young men	Role diffusion, "democracy," younger men have a say
Sex roles in social relationships	Male dominance, machismo	Sex equality

Source: Cultural Access Group based on M. Isabel Valdés, 1990–1994

FIGURE 4.2 _____

Broad Cultural Differences Between Hispanics and the American Middle Class

Hispanics	Anglos
Group oriented ("for my family")	Self oriented ("for me")
Larger families	Smaller families
Lean toward collectivism	Lean toward individualism
Success means family, group satisfaction	Success means personal possessions, individual satisfaction
Stress hierarchies, social class, social stratification, interdependence	Stress equality, "equal rights," democracy, authority, symmetrical relationships, individual autonomy
Doctors and any established source of authority are respected and trusted, and never questioned	Doctors and other established sources of authority may be respected and trusted but often are questioned
At least one daily meal involves elaborate food preparation	Daily meals are usually not prepared from scratch
Believe in fate: pessimists	Believe in self-determination: optimists
Accept delayed gratification	Look for immediate gratification
"High-touch," physical closeness, hugging, affectionate	"High-tech," more physically distant
Spontaneous	Planners
Overt emotions are part of the culture	Hiding emotions is encouraged
Relaxed about time	Adhere to schedules
Very sensitive to fashion	Relaxed about fashion
Pay careful attention to clothing, appearance, hairstyle	Far more relaxed and casual about clothing, appearance, and hairstyle
Longer social protocols, indirect	Brief, to the point, and direct
Adapt to environment	Change the environment
Spiritual, religious things are more important than material things	Material things are more important than spiritual things
Low reliance on institutions	High reliance on institutions
Very decorative in homes	More casual about home decorations
Buy American products	Tend to buy imports
Value highly personal or personalized service	Value fast, efficient service at arm's length
Appreciate being given all the needed time (the more the better) when interacting with service providers	Appreciate efficiency, to the point
Rely more on mutual, implicit understanding	Rely more on explicit language
Tend to prefer prestige brands	Less likely to prefer prestige brands
Tend to live in larger households	Tend to have smaller households
Stress cooperation, participation, being a part of the group	Stress competition, achievement, motivation, self-competence

Source: Cultural Access Group based on M. Isabel Valdés, 1990–1994

THE DANGERS OF STRAIGHT TRANSLATION

Lack of cultural attunement is evident in many translations, including print ads, radio and TV spots, and billboards. It is common to encounter poor translations that are simply incorrect, as well as sophisticated, literal, or academic translations of ads or signs from English into Spanish, where the words are correct but the meaning is not. In addition, there are serious cases of cultural "snafu." A good example of a translation that failed is that of a well-known airline that tried to lure passengers with the phrase *Sentado en cuero*. The original message was intended to emphasize the comfort of sitting on leather seats, but the translation encouraged consumers to "sit naked."

Anybody can learn another language, but learning the emotional connotations and denotations of the words, as well as learning how words are used in a particular culture, is a more difficult and demanding process. To successfully translate a message in any type of communication, be it a TV or radio ad, a print campaign, a brochure, or an outdoor sign, the translation must be culturally relevant, tailored specifically to its intended audience and in the appropriate U.S. Spanish colloquial language. This is easier to do when the cultural origin of the copy- or message-writer or creative team is that of the target audience. This is one of the main reasons why working with Hispanic ad agencies, or creative teams, has a much greater chance of producing successful marketing and communication results.

Working with Hispanic ad agencies, or creative teams, has a much greater chance of producing successful communication results.

Chapter 5

Ongoing Acculturation

Because waves of Hispanic immigrants have come from a variety of countries into different geographic regions at different times, the level of acculturation varies from region to region.

When people immigrate to the United States, they bring with them the "cultural aura" that reflects both their personal lives and that of their home country. Their thoughts and actions start to mingle, little by little, with the culture of the host country, in this case the United States. This is what is referred to as the acculturation process, "the process of integration of native and traditional values with the dominant culture's values" (adapted from Falicov, 1982).

There are several factors affecting the acculturation process, and these can be either external or internal. External factors include, environment, community and geographic location. Internal factors include personality, degree of formal schooling and availability of a support system.

The U.S. Hispanic market is composed of consumers at different stages of acculturation in America. Because waves of Hispanic immigrants have come from a variety of countries into different geographic regions at different times, the level of acculturation varies from region to region as well. In addition, within a family or household, different rates of acculturation may be found; for example, Hispanics who arrived as children or adolescents usually acculturate faster than their foreign-born parents who immigrated as adults or other adults living in the same house, such as grandparents, aunts, and uncles.

ACCULTURATION FACTORS

Many factors affect the pace with which individuals acculturate. There are numerous external factors that play a role, circumstances over which the person has little or no control. For example, the size of the Hispanic community or neighborhood in which the person lives may either accelerate or slow the acculturation process. If the Hispanic community is large, chances are the transition will be slower than if the newly arrived immigrant lives in a predominantly Anglo neighborhood. In other words, high Hispanic population density tends to slow down the acculturation process. If the individual lives and works in a predominantly Anglo environment, then he or she will probably adopt some cultural traits faster. Another external factor that affects the degree of acculturation is the attitude of the community toward the immigrants, the level of acceptance or rejection. If Hispanics are accepted and integrated into American society, rather than isolated, their chances for a faster acculturation process are greater. Acculturation pace also varies according to age. Children and adolescents have a much easier time than adults adapting to new circumstances.

Other factors affecting the nature and speed of acculturation are internal to the individual and include psychological characteristics, educational level, economic status and the presence or absence of personal and family networks. When immigrants are educated, financially stable, surrounded by friends and family familiar with the language or an American support network, they tend to acculturate faster. Finally, some social behaviors and cultural aspects can be assimilated

Other factors affecting the nature and speed of acculturation are internal to the individual and include psychological characteristics, educational level, economic status and the presence or absence of personal and family networks.

faster than others. For example, learning a new language is easier than adopting new values. Core cultural values and beliefs are usually difficult to change. This is true across socioeconomic groups and independent of years of residence in the U.S. or even number of generations living in America (Gordon 1964; Teske and Nelson, as cited in Falicov and Karrer, 1986).

Learning a new language is easier than adopting new values. Core cultural values and beliefs are usually difficult to change.

ACCULTURATION AND INDIVIDUAL TRAITS

Attitude, personality, and reasons for migration also affect a person's transition from one culture to another. For instance, the expectations and aspirations of an immigrant who came to the United States "to escape poverty or unemployment" will tend to differ from those of the highly skilled or professionally trained immigrant who fled political persecution. The former chose to leave friends, family and a known world for better working opportunities, whereas the latter might have preferred to stay in his or her home country but was compelled to leave for survival reasons. Similarly, the immigrant child brought to the United States by his or her parents may have a very different set of values, expectations and experiences altogether than someone who immigrated at an older age or on their own.

Foreign-born, first-generation individuals and families who move to the United States could be described as the pioneers. They tend to be more innovative and less passive than relatives who come to join them later or second-generation siblings and children who are born in the United States.

RETRO-ACCULTURATION

Retro-acculturation, a term coined by marketing researcher Carlos E. Garcia, refers to the conscious search for ethnic identity or roots, especially by second-, third- or fourth-generation Mexican Americans who have lost some or most of their cultural traits. These individuals tend to be highly assimilated into mainstream American culture yet would like to enjoy and recover the culture of their parents and grandparents. A well-known example is the singer Linda Ronstadt, with the traditional Mexican *corridos* in her album, *Songs from My Father*.

Hispanics who choose retro-acculturation typically want to learn Spanish, have their children learn Spanish, and appreciate their cultural heritage (values, music, arts, food and so on). They are proud of their heritage and welcome ethnic recognition in advertising and promotion of brands and services. As consumers, they may patronize brands that target Hispanics, or may watch Spanish-language TV and listen to Spanish-language programming. They also tend to support Hispanic-related activities, purchase Spanish-language newspapers, and vote for Hispanic candidates. A sense of ethnic identity and pride tends to motivate these behaviors. This subsegment of the Hispanic market is growing steadily as the Latino middle class continues to grow.

Hispanics who choose retro-acculturation typically want to learn Spanish, have their children learn Spanish, and appreciate their cultural heritage.

A TRADITIONAL CULTURE

Some cultural traits, values and expressions of these behaviors are prominent and different in the Hispanic culture. In order to understand Hispanic culture, you must first become familiar with the following four concepts: *familismo*, relationships with children, *machismo* and *marianismo*.

Familismo

The pillar of Hispanic culture is the family, which includes the extended family of grandparents, uncles, aunts and cousins. The emphasis Hispanics place on

The family's needs and welfare take precedence over the individual member's needs.

relatives has been called *familismo*. The family's needs and welfare take precedence over the individual member's needs. The family, as a group, is usually the first and only priority. This is reflected in the educational process within the family as well as in the family's expectations toward each other.

"Parents are viewed as being obliged to make all sorts of sacrifices for the children. As a response, the child is expected to show gratitude, for example, assuming responsibility for younger siblings and for the parents in old age. . . . The child internalizes at an early age the overwhelming and powerful role of the parents and the family; the mother tends to define herself as an individual mostly in terms of her family. The father enjoys more freedom, but he is responsible for the respectful behavior of his children, and feels morally responsible for the behavior of the whole family." (Falcon, 1972).

It is not surprising, then, that so much Spanish-language advertising strategy revolves around the family, either explicitly or implicitly.

Relationships with Children

A major difference between mainstream American and traditional Hispanic cultures is in child-rearing orientations. "Children [in Hispanic families] are not believed to be capable of acting independently until they reach maturity . . . regardless of the physical and emotional development of the child. This leads to parental over-concern for keeping the child close and attached to the family." (Falcon, 1972).

This dependency affects the child's decision-making process in purchases and, hence, the marketing and advertising strategy. Even the most basic children's products, such as cereals and toys, benefit from including the mother (or another adult) in the creative strategy in order to "close the sale more effectively."

Machismo

Machismo is a complex set of beliefs, attitudes, values, and behaviors about the role of men that is pervasive in Hispanic culture. The concept refers to the roles men fulfill according to societal rules and how they view themselves with respect to their environment and other people. It goes beyond how men treat women in stereotypically dominating ways, such as being "macho." It involves how men function as providers, protectors and representatives of their families to the outer world. They have obligations and responsibilities to uphold the honor of the family members, to deal effectively with the public sphere and to maintain the integrity of the family unit. *Machismo* also refers to having socially acceptable, manly characteristics, such as being courageous, strong, and virile. The manly image includes being seen as the head of the household, but listening to and being respectful of women. This traditional role provides much more freedom for men than women with regard to sexual activity and public, social interactions.

Marianismo

Marianismo is, to some extent, the female counterpart of machismo. The term refers to an excessive sense of self-sacrifice found among traditional and less acculturated Hispanic women—the more sacrifice, the better mother, the better spouse—many times to the detriment of the woman. This cultural trait is supported by a complex set of deep-rooted beliefs and values that determine how Hispanic women choose to live, or better said, not to live their lives. Cultural Access research has found that many Hispanic women do not go, or postpone going, to the doctor even when they feel sick because they "need to take care of the children and the house." Often, a Hispanic woman does not feel she has the right to ask her spouse to cover for her. In her frame of mind, this would be considered "selfish."

Marianismo has both positive and negative aspects. The positive aspects are key to the Hispanic family. They include being a very dedicated, loving and supportive wife and mother, teaching the children Hispanic culture and religion, being a *comadre* (godmother, friend) in the community, and being highly empathetic and ready to help those

Marianismo is not helping young Latinas become healthy members of society.

in need. However, the impact of the negative aspects of *marianismo* affects many social and marketing realities. *Marianismo* tends to breed low self-esteem and depression, which limits a Latina's personal potential.

From a marketing perspective, these non-acculturated Latina women trail behind their male counterparts in their English-language skills. They tend not to spend money on themselves, even if it is money that they themselves earn. *Marianismos'* problems are particularly serious among non-acculturated young newlywed women and recent immigrants. Our research has found a higher incidence of low self-esteem and depression in the latter segment. One study conducted for a telephone service company showed that a significant number of young Latina women in Chicago spent many hours on the phone, running up high long-distance and international phone bills in search of emotional support from relatives left behind.

Marianismo is not helping young Latinas become healthy members of society. Latina teen pregnancy is on the rise, and low self-esteem is rampant in lower socioeconomic groups. In 1998, The National Coalition of Hispanic Health and Human Services Organization, which closely tracks Latino health-related issues, conducted a study among Hispanic girls aged 9 to 12 and their parents (COSSMHO, 1998). Its findings show that "the prevalence of health risk behaviors such as suicide attempts, substance use, and teenage pregnancy" is pervasive among Latina teens. These findings are consistent with existing data on the subject. Living in two cultures while having to cope with stress and non-flattering feminine role models, in both the household and the community, are challenges that the new Latina teen is presently facing. A healthier image is slowly emerging and is discussed in Marketing to the "New Latina" in chapter 6.

Cultural Characteristics at a Glance . . .

The following traits tend to be prevalent among more traditional, and/or non-acculturated, Hispanic adults and foreign-borns. Variations do exist among the various Hispanic subgroups.

- Speak Spanish at home

- Mostly Catholic, but Mormons and Protestants increasing; other religious practices include *Santeria* and *Espiritism* (very limited)

- Status-oriented professionals like to be addressed with respect (e.g., Mr., Mrs.) and by their title (e.g., doctor, architect, professor, minister or padre)

- Family-oriented

- Group-oriented

- Family stratified by sex and age—father, mother, children

- Generational hierarchy—grandparents, children, grandchildren

- Observant in social interaction based on authority and familiarity of the parties involved

- Amicable but formal in business situations—last names preferred; addressing a new client by his or her first name is rarely welcome

- Respectful of social graces, especially with regard to women and the elderly. A pecking order exists; recognizing and showing respect to the older person present is always welcomed

- More focused on the present rather than the future, and live the phrase, *¡Dios Dira!* (God will tell!)

Chapter 6

Marketing in a Bicultural Context

Scholars in the field of communication have found that successful communication takes place if, and only if, the message generator/sender (the advertiser, the marketer, any communicator) uses the same codes (language, symbols, images) as the decoder/receiver (the customer, client, patient, voter).

Regardless of the size of the audience—ten people or a million—the message is always decoded, received and understood on an individual basis. In today's message-cluttered world, marketers and advertisers cannot expect their audiences to work hard at decoding and understanding their messages. It must be the opposite. The message must be culturally and linguistically fine-tuned, that is "in-culture," delivered within a context and tonality that is acceptable and familiar to the receiver, so that it is transparent and understood without any interference.

Communication, including advertising, marketing and promotion, always takes place within a cultural, social context. Effective bicultural communication and marketing build on cultural awareness and cultural sensitivity. This awareness is key to understanding the mind-set of the consumer and must be used from the conceptualization stage of the message to strategic planning, final implementation and execution.

The meaning of the message can change drastically

in a bicultural environment. There is a feeling of "communications safety" that people acquire from having lived in the same country and having shared cultural experiences. For example, in the United States, most people know about Babe Ruth, the symbol of American baseball, and why he became so famous. Anywhere on the planet, one American can say to another, "My son is the next Babe Ruth," and the other person would understand the message. No explanations are needed. But if the same remark were made to a Mexican or South American, that person would most likely stare at the other wondering who this babe named Ruth is. Chances are that more "acculturated" Hispanics, and certainly Puerto Ricans or Cubans, who have made substantial contributions to American baseball would understand the full meaning of the comment. Others may not.

The basic principles used in communicating with consumers apply to any market. If messages in the general market are continually refined to convey clarity of expression and to match the emergent images in American culture, the same approach can and should be used to target Hispanics, or any other ethnic group. A culturally attuned approach should be followed each step of the way—from conceptualization and strategic planning through final implementation and execution, as indicated in **Figure 6.1**.

The cultural approach to marketing to Hispanics is not new; it has been used in the past. Specialists in the Hispanic market, usually Hispanics, have implemented successful marketing campaigns that have made hefty contributions to the bottom line of their clients. Unfortunately, marketing and advertising budgets are often too small to reap the great potential offered by this market. What is needed now is a new look at the business opportunities and budgetary reallocations to meet the marketing challenges of this rapidly growing market.

Two books were recently released by eminent Latinos, helping the new generations learn how to acculturate and succeed in America. Advertising legend and president of Garcia/LKS, an advertising agency in San Antonio, Texas, Lionel Sosa encourages Latinos while telling his own story in *The Americano Dream* (Penguin Group, 1998). In his book, a Mexican-American life journey, Lionel shares a compelling story of what it was—and sometimes still is—like to be a Mexican immigrant in America and to succeed in business.

FIGURE 6.1 _____

Checklist for a Culturally Attuned Communication Process

Message Sender ("Coder")

All elements in a culturally attuned message should be in consonance with the receiver's culture:

- Ad's text (copy)
- People shown (talent)
- Non-verbal cues
- Symbols and metaphors
- Music
- Setting or location
- Interaction between people
- Acting (body language, speech, accent, apparel)
- Pace and tonality
- Product and message context
- Emotional codes

Medium

Language (English or Spanish) and frequency should be that which is closest to the target audience's "heart" (emotions) and everyday behavior. For example, if they watch, listen, or read in Spanish most of the time, the number of ads or commercials should be in proportion to their use of that specific language.

Message Receiver ("Decoder")

If all elements are in consonance with the receiver's culture, the receiver will perceive the message as "talking to me, in my own culture," and the message will not draw attention to itself.

1. A bilingual consumer has language choices. However, the Hispanic "cultural" component of the message is constant in both languages. The more "in-culture," the greater the chance of recall and effectiveness.

2. An English-dominant Hispanic consumer may also respond more effectively to Hispanic "in-culture" messages.

Source: Cultural Access Group, based on Ogilvy, 1964; M. Isabel Valdés, 1990–2000

After years of professional practice in New York City, Dr. Carmen Vasquez and Dr. Rosa Maria Gil—an extraordinary pair of psychologists of Dominican and Cuban origin—unveiled in their book, *The Maria Paradox,* a tool to help Latinos integrate cultural traditions with a North American way of life. They will help you truly grasp the core—the heart—of U.S. Latino marketing.

SELECTING YOUR LATINO MARKET SEGMENT

The Latino market is a moving target. By the time a foreign-born Latino becomes "savvy" about the value of coupons or health, car or life insurance, or diet products, many thousands more have arrived and need to be informed that coupons exist, the value of various types of insurance products, and the importance of a healthy diet. Chances are both the "savvy" group and the newcomers would need—or prefer—to be communicated with in Spanish. Simultaneously, another growing segment of the Hispanic market, born in the United States, always knew about coupons, the value of insurance, and the importance of a healthy diet. Chances are they would much rather be approached in English and certainly not as if they have never seen a coupon in their lives.

How do you target this moving market? How do you seize the opportunity? Which of these segments presents a better business opportunity for your specific product or service category? Should you communicate in English or Spanish with your Hispanic customers?

A simple method to help you think about these strategic issues is to analyze them on the basis of a generational view of the U.S. Latino market. By separating U.S.-born versus foreign-born Hispanics in your marketing analysis and visualizing the product or category within their experiences as consumers, this complex dilemma disappears. To do this, you must ask a sample of your customers for some basic information. Ask, "In what country were you born?" and if born outside the U.S., then, "How old were you when you migrated to the United States?" The answers to these questions can help you create or add a very powerful market intelligence layer to your customer database and marketing plan. You can know what percentage of your current customer database is acculturated since you can easily calculate how many were born in the United States (and hence, speak English fluently) and what percentage has resided in the U.S. only a year or two. You will find out how many arrived as adults and will probably not be as familiar with your product, service or retail chain.

In other words, the marketing and communications strategies to successfully target each of these three Hispanic market segments will need to be in consonance with the degree of acculturation and exposure to mainstream American culture and marketing practices. (See more on this in chapters 8 and 9.)

Now, how do you decide which of these unique market segments should be the focus of your Hispanic marketing strategy? A generational analysis (**Figure 6.2**) of the Hispanic population, based on U.S. Census Bureau projections, provides an answer to this question.

FIGURE 6.2

Generational Diversity

(millions)

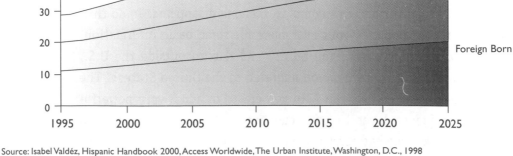

Source: Isabel Valdéz, Hispanic Handbook 2000, Access Worldwide, The Urban Institute, Washington, D.C., 1998

A simple visual review of the generational figure tells a compelling story regarding the potential of the overall U.S. Hispanic market. It also provides insight into its different sub-groups including the U.S.-born segment that will more than triple in the next decades and the foreign-born segment that will continue growing and contributing to the U.S. population for many decades. Presently, the greatest business opportunity for most products and services is found by targeting foreign-born Latinos. There are brand-new households to furnish, electronics to be acquired, cars to be purchased, children to be clothed, and mouths to be fed. Latino households can be easily targeted via Spanish-language media, with unique (e.g., introductory, educational) campaigns in Spanish.

The Latino baby boom is another example of an important business opportunity to the foreign-born segment. In the future—and today for some products and services—the business opportunity will be equal or greater than with U.S.-born Latinos because these Hispanic households will have higher incomes and be more savvy with financial tools. Targeting them in-culture will provide an additional competitive edge, similar to target marketing to African Americans today, with unique culturally attuned campaigns.

However, the emerging U.S.–born in-cultural and bilingual generations of Latinos are already here as children, teenagers and young adults, influencing their parents regarding household purchases. Computers, Internet services, cars, amusement parks, food and beverages, electronics and telecommunications are just some examples of categories where this powerful in-culture, acculturated segment impacts the purchases of their often foreign-born parents. It makes sense then that communications strategies include them as "vectors" or influencers to generate a sale.

Two bi-cultural, acculturated segments that should be the focus of U.S.-born Latino marketing in the next decade are Generation Ñ and the New Latina. The sections later in this chapter describe their unique cultures.

The Urban Institute in Washington, D.C. publishes a report every other year with the data necessary to conduct generational longitudinal analyses of the U.S. Hispanic population.

THE LATINO BABY BOOM

Between 1997 and 2001, an estimated 18.6 million babies will be born in the United States. More than one in six of them (nearly 3.3 million) will be born to a Latino mom. Since Latinos reside in a small handful of cities, births to Latino women, on a per-market basis, are dramatically high. (**Figure 6.3**).

FIGURE 6.3

Five-year Projected Births to Hispanic Women by Markets, 1997–2001

Urban areas are sorted according to the percentage of births to Hispanic women from the highest percentage to the lowest.

MSAs and CMSAs	Births to All Women	Births to Hispanic Women	Hispanic Births as % of Total
El Paso	84,445	69,260	82.0%
San Antonio	132,240	86,459	65.4
Los Angeles	1,343,969	708,441	52.7
San Diego	221,728	80,689	36.4
Miami	259,894	94,079	36.2
Houston	372,157	131,540	35.3
San Francisco	438,795	122,473	27.9
New York	1,302,985	341,182	26.2
Dallas	381,808	96,085	25.2
Denver	164,485	39,712	24.0
Sacramento	114,284	24,635	21.6
Chicago	708,522	144,137	20.3
National Total	**18,595,280**	**3,286,974**	**17.7**
Portland	149,645	15,141	10.1
Milwaukee	114,864	9,844	8.6
Philadelphia	380,809	30,195	7.9
Washington, DC	476,856	34,678	7.3
Seattle	221,385	14,479	6.5
Cleveland	189,117	7,210	3.8
Detroit	343,829	12,823	3.7
Cincinnati	130,265	1,246	1.0

Source: Cultural Access Worldwide, TGE Demographics, 1998

Latino births as a percentage of all births can be as high as 53 to 82 percent in high-density Hispanic markets. For example, in the Los Angeles CMSA (which includes Los Angeles, Riverside and Orange County), 53 percent of the newborns will be Hispanic. In other words, more than one of every two children born in the largest Hispanic market in the U.S. will be of Hispanic origin or descent. The fastest-growing Hispanic baby market segments are El Paso and San Antonio with 82 percent and 65 percent Hispanic births, respectively. Cities that have previously not been known for their Hispanic populations are also experiencing the Latino baby boom. This will be most notable in cities such as Portland, Oregon, Milwaukee, Wisconsin, and Washington, DC.

Latinos spend more per child than the non-Hispanic population.

A Latino baby boom means business because Latinos spend more per child than the non-Hispanic population. Known for "over-indulging" their children, Latino parents emphasize giving their children what they did not have. Because Hispanic households are more likely to be larger and to have several generations living together, marketers can reach more people through fewer households.

A study of Hispanic household spending conducted by Cultural Access Group and ACNielsen, among bilingual and English-dominant households from the Homescan Consumer Panel, showed that market penetration for baby foods was 57 percent higher in Hispanic homes than in non-Hispanic homes. This is just one example. Homescan Consumer Panel produces many more.

Because the Hispanic market is more family oriented than the general market, it is not enough to translate general market strategies into Spanish. Marketing must focus on the cultural context and the resulting attitudes that Latinos have toward their children. The pillar of the Hispanic culture is the family, which often includes grandparents, uncles, aunts, cousins and family friends.

It is for this reason that the majority of Spanish-language advertising strategies revolve around the family, either explicitly or implicitly. When marketing even a most basic product to Hispanic children, advertisers should also include a parent (or another adult) in order to make the greatest impact.

HISPANIC YOUTH OR GENERATION Ñ

Generation Ñ includes pre-teens, teens, and young adults. Although they are generally bilingual and open to adapting to the American way of life, they don't want to lose their Hispanic cultural identity (**Figure 6.4**). They navigate comfortably in both cultures, enjoy music in both languages, watch both English and Spanish-language television, and like other youth segments at present, tend to be cynical about tradition. In their hearts, however, there is a great need to belong and be an integral part of America.

During this decade, the U.S. Census Bureau projects the Anglo youth population (under age 18) will decrease 6 percent, while their

FIGURE 6.4

The Best of Both Worlds

"I feel that 50 years from now, Latinos in this country will lose their (Spanish) language and become like everybody else in the U.S."

% Agree

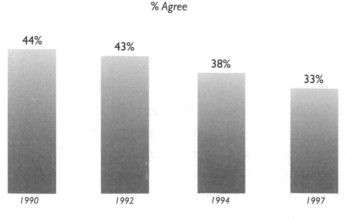

Source: Yankelovich Hispanic MONITOR 1997

Hispanic counterparts will grow by over 25 percent. By 2005, Hispanic youths will be the largest ethnic youth population (**Figure 6.5**).

All segments of the Latino youth market will grow over the next four years, but the most dramatic growth in the Hispanic youth population, will be among Hispanic pre-teens and teens. Between 1998 and 2003, the Hispanic pre-teen segment, aged 10 to 14, will experience 27 percent growth and the teen segment, aged 15 to 19, will grow by 15 percent (**Figure 6.6**).

Presently, Hispanics under age 20 represent 58 percent of all Los

FIGURE 6.5

Total U.S. Youth Under Age 18, 2000–2010

(in thousands)

	2000	2005	2010	% Change 2000–2010
Anglo (non-Hispanic)	45,376	44,208	42,738	-6%
Hispanic	11,033	12,467	13,741	25
African American	11,268	11,792	12,153	8
Asian	3,299	3,816	4,304	30

Source: U.S. Census Bureau, 1998

FIGURE 6.6

Hispanic Youth Population, 1998–2003

(in thousands)

	1998	2003	% Change 1998–2003
Under age 5	3,133	3,419	9.1%
5–9 years	3,127	3,296	5.4
10–14 years	2,664	3,383	27.0
15–19 years	2,576	2,974	15.5
Total	11,500	13,072	13.7

Source: TGE Demographics, 1998

Angeles youth under 20. This group and will grow to capture 80 percent by 2003. From 1998 to 2003, the fastest-growing Hispanic youth population will be the Dallas-Fort Worth area where the Hispanic children and teens population will increase 21 percent from 1998 to 2003. Not far behind will be Miami and Houston, whose Hispanic youth populations will grow by 19 percent and 18 percent, respectively, in the same period (**Figure 6.7**).

FIGURE 6.7

Total Hispanic Youth, 1998–2003

(aged 0 to 19, by metro area)

Metro	1998	2003	Change	% Change
Los Angeles CMSA	2,476,505	2,775,022	298,517	12%
New York (NY-NJ-CT-PA) CMSA	1,180,153	1,327,367	147,214	12
Chicago (IL-IN-WI) CMSA	484,497	549,785	65,288	13
San Francisco-Oakland-San Jose CMSA	467,913	523,558	55,645	12
Houston CMSA	438,878	517,249	78,371	18
Miami CMSA	364,632	434,159	69,527	19
San Antonio MSA	313,081	361,320	48,239	15
Dallas-Fort Worth CMSA	307,157	372,734	65,577	21
San Diego MSA	280,279	317,126	36,847	13
El Paso MSA	211,397	246,196	34,799	16

Source: TGE Demographics, 1998

As the Hispanic youth market becomes the largest, and remains one of the fastest-growing ethnic youth segments, it will offer a wealth of business potential across categories of products and services. Hispanics tend to spend more on their children than do Anglo-Americans, and this is also true for teenagers. A recent study of Hispanic household spending conducted by Cultural Access Worldwide and ACNielsen showed that market penetration for items typically purchased by and for children and teenagers, such as crayons, gum, acne medication, cosmetics and soft-drinks, was an average of 38 percent higher in Hispanic than non-Hispanic homes.

MARKETING TO HISPANIC YOUTH—THERE IS A DIFFERENCE

Obviously, a child or a teenager is a child or teenager in any culture. Hispanic teens follow developmental stages like any other teen in the world. Teens want to identify with their peer group. They want to look like and behave like their friends at school or in the *barrio*. But marketers should not assume that strategies used to target youth in the general market will work with Hispanic teens as well. Many Hispanic teens are not only influenced by their peers, but also by Hispanic culture, and the process of acculturation. These factors, which are not present among general market youth, have a strong effect on the way Hispanic teens relate to spending and decision making.

Culturally, Hispanic teenagers are raised to be closer, more dependent on their parents, and for as long as possible. As a result, Hispanic children tend to start primary school later and live at home longer than their Anglo counterparts. *Familismo,* or strong family orientation, is an important Hispanic cultural value which is forged and reinforced during Hispanic children's lives. *Familismo* plays an important role throughout their lives, impacting how they interact with friends, relatives and the community at large. As a result, the Hispanic parent tends to have a stronger influence in the child's purchasing and decision making.

The acculturation process adds another dimension to the Hispanic child development task. In most cases, Generation Ñ lives between two cultures, adding new roles and expectations that result in sources of positive self-image and aspirations, as well as adding additional pressure and anxiety. This situation is particularly true among Spanish-Only parent households where the child is the "bilingual communicator." The child many times has to act as translator and go-between to help in adult decision-making. This can include purchases of durable goods, selections of brands and products, or translating at the physician's office for the parents.

On the positive side, bilingual children and teens act as "acculturation factors" who can boost their own self-esteem by introducing their parents to new products, and by helping their parents locate the products they are looking for in the store or supermarket. In this case, the youngster can play an important role in the decision-making process and can be considered a "partner" in marketing and advertising strategies. On the other hand, the bilingual household can generate more anxiety when Spanish-Only parents feel at a loss, dependent on the child's help, and unable to play their roles as the adults. In this situation, parents may feel not in control of their children's lives.

In studies with Spanish-Only parents of bilingual teenagers, Cultural Access Group has observed that English-language media can be perceived as a threat because parents cannot understand nor control what their bilingual or English-Only children are watching. Parents in these households will either limit their children's exposure to English-language media, or sit through it, trying to understand and control what their children are watching. Conversely, these parents influence and sometimes pressure their children to watch Spanish-language television with them. Watching Spanish-language television then becomes a relaxed, high-quality family time activity, where the family shares not only the fun, but also their Spanish-language and Hispanic culture and values.

English-language media can be perceived as a threat by Spanish-Only parents of bilingual teenagers, because parents cannot understand nor control what their bilingual or English Only children are watching.

COMMUNICATING WITH LATINO YOUTH

Because cultural nuances can make the difference between a successful, profitable marketing campaign and one that is not, cultural fine-tuning is needed when marketing to Hispanic youth, even in English. From creative development to merchandising to research, marketing needs to include both acculturated and non-acculturated children or teenagers and their parents. Careful attention needs to be placed on the family-centered nature of the Hispanic culture, and how the acculturation process impacts a particular product, service or media program. Because of the varying degrees of acculturation within a Hispanic family, a Spanish-Only or English-Only strategy may not be effective in reaching the Hispanic youth market. A cross-over communication strategy may be the best option.

Spanish? English? Bilingual? Depending on your product and strategy presentation, all of the above are viable languages to successfully reach U.S. Hispanic youth. Because so many Hispanic youths are born and raised in the United States today, the Spanish-Only strategy may not be as effective as it used to be to impact Hispanic children and teens. The Hispanic Baby Boom is mostly composed of Latino children and teens that tend to be bilingual and bicultural. Their fluency in Spanish will depend mostly on parental interaction and pressure to communicate in Spanish, both in the household and neighborhood. The higher the Hispanic density, the greater the chance they will interact with their peers at school, at church, and in the *barrio* in Spanish. Hence, the decision to communicate in one language or another will depend mainly on the type of product or service being marketed and the dynamics at the core of the family. Even though today's Hispanic children and teens may be fully bilingual or English preferred, their parents, the final decision makers, may be foreign born and are more effectively reached and impacted in their native language, Spanish, even if they have become bilingual.

To decide which is the appropriate or "most effective" language, several factors need to be carefully weighed, including the ages of the targets, U.S. born versus foreign born, the marketing strategy, and the product or service to be marketed. Is it milk? Or telephone services? Or cars? If the product or service requires high parental approval or intervention, such as food, phones and cars, a two-tiered strategy may be advisable. The parents may be targeted in Spanish and the teens in a cross-over or a bilingual strategy (via Spanish or English-language media). It will be the actual content of the television show, radio program, or print media that will capture the teens' attention, independent of language.

The letter Ñ is symbolic, and unique to the Spanish-language, hence, a common denominator among the estimated 420 million Spanish-speaking people around the globe.

MARKETING TO GENERATION Ñ

Machismo and *marianismo* will be "a thing of the past" to the many young Latinos that compose the fast-growing Generation Ñ. "Ñ" as a Hispanic cultural icon was coined by Hispanic strategist and advertising guru Victoria Hudson and her agency, Cartel Creativo. While researching a name for a new digital multiplex channel targeting Latinos, they selected Canales ñ. The letter Ñ is symbolic, and unique to the Spanish-language, hence, a common denominator among the estimated 420 million Spanish-speaking people around the globe.

In today's Hispanic marketing environment, Generation Ñ is also symbolic of a young, positive and energetic Latino market segment, ready to move into the world successfully. This is the generation inspired, groomed and supported by successful Hispanics, and visionaries who have embraced the value of a multicultural society.

MARKETING TO THE "NEW LATINA"

FIGURE 6.8

The "New Latina," although still shaking off some of the characteristics of *marianismo,* is, to some degree, the opposite of the *marianista*. In their book *The Maria Paradox*, Drs. Gil and Vazquez present strategies for Latinas to merge "old-world traditions" with "new-world self-esteem." Their Ten Commandments of Marianismo provide clear and practical comparisons showing where the Latina soul is coming from, and where it wants to go. The transition from the old "ways" to the new is most pressing for young Hispanic women today. The September 1999 issue of *Latina* magazine **(Figure 6.8)**— a magazine specifically designed to talk to the heart of the new Latina—addresses the battle of the young Latina interviewed: "All I wanted was to be myself." She could not escape her parent's daily control, even after she had completed college. The new Latina woman wants to succeed in business and at home with her family, live in both cultures, and make it in America.

The fastest-growing segment among first-time employed persons are Latina women. These women are an important factor contributing to the ongoing income growth of the Hispanic household as shown in **Figure 6.9**. Every income group has increased significantly, not only in absolute numbers, but also percentage-wise. This consistent growth across income segments confirms more Hispanic households are making more money, often times contributed by the female head of the house getting a job. Today Latinas are found at every level of corporate America. They are taking positions as general laborers, nurses, computer technicians, attorneys, doctors, CEOs, and small-business managers **(Figure 6.10)**.

FIGURE 6.9

Income Growth

Constant (1996) Dollars

	1985		1996		1985–1996	
	Number (000)	Percent	Number (000)	Percent	Change (000)	Percent Change
$100,000 or more	93	2.0%	417	4.6%	323	346.6%
$75,000–$99,999	196	4.2	507	5.6	311	158.9
$50,000–$74,999	583	12.5	1,268	14.0	685	117.5
$35,000–$49,999	784	16.8	1,431	15.8	648	82.6
$25,000–$34,999	737	15.8	1,477	16.3	740	100.3
$15,000–$24,999	896	19.2	1,622	17.9	726	81.0
Under $15,000	1,376	29.5	2,377	25.8	961	69.8
Total	**4,666**	**100.0**	**9,060**	**100.0**	**4,394**	**94.2**
Average Income	31,661	—	38,280	—	6,619	20.9
Aggregate Income (billions)	147,730	—	346,817	—	199,087	134.8

Source: TGE Demographics estimates based on U.S. Census Bureau's Current Population Survey data

FIGURE 6.10

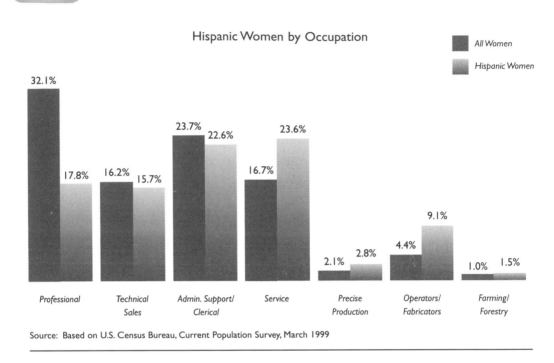

Hispanic Women by Occupation

■ *All Women*

■ *Hispanic Women*

| Professional | Technical Sales | Admin. Support/ Clerical | Service | Precise Production | Operators/ Fabricators | Farming/ Forestry |

32.1% / 17.8% | 16.2% / 15.7% | 23.7% / 22.6% | 16.7% / 23.6% | 2.1% / 2.8% | 4.4% / 9.1% | 1.0% / 1.5%

Source: Based on U.S. Census Bureau, Current Population Survey, March 1999

In sum, the New Latina is leaving her mark in every field—politics, business, academia and the arts. However, she continues leaving a mark with her family and the community by regularly making time to have dinner with the whole family and by volunteering for the community and those in need. The family and social connections are still very strong. This is reflected also in the purchase behavior, for example, of beepers and cellular phones, which are used to connect several times a day with children and spouse. Hispanic household phone bills are consistently much higher across income segments than those of non-Hispanic households. Most of the calls placed are to parents and siblings—at least on a monthly basis—resulting in very high international phone bills.

The New Latina market is composed of about 10 million women (aged 18 and older). **Figure 6.11** shows that as a group, the New Latina is younger on average than other American women. As consumers, they are very active in the marketplace, purchasing cars, clothes, personal-care products, insurance and financial products, and opening bank accounts. They are learning to navigate the Internet, traveling, and helping their families purchase homes.

FIGURE 6.11

Projected Median Age of U.S. Women

Persons of Hispanic origin may be of any race.

	2000	2005	2010
Hispanic	28	29	30
Non-Hispanic White	40	41	42
Black / not Hispanic	32	33	33
Asian / not Hispanic	32	33	34

Source: Based on U.S. Bureau of the Census; in M.I. Valdés & Seoane, *Hispanic Market Handbook*, Gale Research, 1995

Although to a lesser degree than the previous generation, Latinas today enjoy cooking from scratch not only out of nostalgia, but to please a husband and parents. However, the use of practical, ready-to-eat items has significantly penetrated the Hispanic household, in some cases surpassing the average household consumption. Today, cereal, which is not part of traditional Hispanic cuisine, is consumed regularly and in large quantities (Hispanic Homescan Panel, Los Angeles Test, 1999).

The use of practical, ready-to-eat items has significantly penetrated the Hispanic household.

In comparison with the traditional Hispanic woman, New Latinas are much more likely to indulge in clothes, accessories, makeup, personal-care products, perfumes, and other self-pampering goods and services.

Lastly, New Latinas are great consumers of American music and popular culture. At the same time, their Latin culture is a source of pride and enjoyment. No party would be a party without Latin music and foods, and there is a great variety of Latin music available today, from the newest *merengue, salsa,* or hip-hop, to the traditional *mariachi* tunes in a new incarnation.

The Latina's acculturation into mainstream American culture is increasing every day. Latina women are leaving home before marriage to go to college, to work, travel, or just "find themselves." They do this to the great chagrin of parents, who would like to see them dressed in white before they fly from the nest.

Marketing to the New Latina, as well as marketing to Generation Ñ, will pose many challenges for service companies and manufacturers in the new millennium. A great number of media vehicles are presently available in both Spanish and English, from newspapers and magazines, to radio and television, to the Internet. Choosing the appropriate strategy and medium requires in-depth knowledge of this unique and growing Hispanic market segment.

Chapter 7

Gaining "Share of Heart"

I n the mid-1980s, two highly successful Hispanic advertisers, Hector and Norma Orci, developed a Hispanic marketing presentation entitled "To Sell Me Is to Know Me." Based on their keen observations of the key barriers to successful Hispanic marketing they concluded: "It has to do with truly knowing the consumer and knowing how to gain 'share of heart'," not just share of mind. The following paragraphs will focus on how to gain Hispanic consumer insight and "share of heart."

To position a product or service effectively, you must ensure that the message is clear and free from stereotypes, myths, preconceptions, ambivalence and potentially negative interpretations. In other words, the message must be perceived by the receiver as if he or she had designed it. The portrayal of a Mexican riding a burro and wearing a sombrero is an example of poor cultural sensitivity and lack of factual information. The burro and sombrero may well communicate Mexico to a non-Mexican audience, but not to a Mexican or Mexican-American one. Anyone of Mexican descent will most certainly perceive this image as an indirect insult, one that says "you and your countrymen are backward." Such popular stereotypes regarding Hispanic consumers should be avoided to prevent delivering negatively charged messages.

To position a product or service effectively, you must ensure that the message is clear and free from stereotypes, myths, preconceptions, ambivalence, and potentially negative interpretations.

AVOIDING STEREOTYPES

A stereotype is a set of generalizations about a group or category of people that is usually unfavorable, exaggerated, and oversimplified. Most stereotypes tend to emphasize negative qualities, are emotionally charged, and are difficult to change even in the face of empirical evidence (adopted from Theodorson and Theodorson, 1970). Stereotypes, such as the Mexican wearing the sombrero and riding a burro, have the potential to irritate and disrupt the flow of healthy and effective communication between marketers and consumers and should be eliminated from any marketing communications.

Latinos, like most people, dislike being labeled and placed in cubbyholes.

Latinos, like most people, dislike being labeled and placed in cubbyholes. When a consumer perceives an unfavorable portrayal, the immediate response is that the message was not created or executed by someone like himself. At that instant, the golden rule of successful communication—the message must be perceived to have come from "someone like me"—is broken. In a matter of seconds, the viewer's attention is diverted from the core message to the false or stereotyped image presented in the ad. As viewers become trapped in a tangle of miscommunication, they will not only miss the core message; they will walk away from the product and the sponsor.

Symbols used in stereotypical messages, whether images, music, slang or talent, are not the ones the people being stereotyped would choose to view themselves or to communicate with each other. Avoiding such stereotypes is easier than it may appear. It is a two-step process. First, marketers must be aware that some of the perceptions people hold about others who may not look or speak like them do not hold up in the face of reality. Second, a "reality check" (e.g., qualitative research) is recommended at all stages of the marketing plan.

Most stereotypes about Hispanics tend to stress race and socioeconomic issues, often placing Hispanics at the low end of the socioeconomic scale. If these stereotypes were accepted at face value, one might ask, why bother targeting consumers who have no money and no potential to make any?

The following are stereotypes to avoid:

Stereotype 1: Hispanics are seen as farmworkers with no money no future, and no ambition.

U.S. Hispanics are the wealthiest Latin-American consumers in the Americas. As illustrated in **Figure 7.1**, the income per capita of U.S. Hispanics is several times that of the oil-exporting Latin-American countries of Mexico ($4,360) and Venezuela ($3,164). By all criteria, the more than 31.4 million U.S. Hispanics present a stronger and better opportunity for businesses.

Contrary to popular belief, U.S. Hispanics are more likely to live in metropolitan areas than non-Hispanics. Only 8 percent of Hispanics live in non-metropolitan areas, whereas 23 percent of non-Hispanics do, according to the Census Bureau. The vast majority of Hispanics —92 percent—reside in metropolitan areas. Forty-four percent live in the suburbs within metropolitan areas, while 48 percent live in central cities.

Although Hispanics are overrepresented in craft, labor, and farm occupations, the vast majority work in nonfarm activities. In 1990, for example, only about 8 percent of employed Hispanics in California were farm laborers, with the rest employed in managerial and professional positions (11.7 percent); sales, administrative, and technical support areas (21.8 percent); service jobs (19.4 percent); precision and craft workers (13 percent); and operator and laborer positions (25.8 percent).

Hispanics work hard and frequently work in more than one occupation. Like

FIGURE 7.1

U.S. and Selected Latin-American Countries Hispanic Income per Capita

1998 dollars

	US$ 1990	US$ 1998
U.S. Hispanics	$9,204	$12,557**
Puerto Rico	6,470*	8,600
Venezuela	2,560	3,164
Uruguay	2,560	6,000
Mexico	2,490	4,360
Argentina	2,370	9,100
Chile	1,940	4,922
Costa Rica	1,910	2,900
El Salvador	1,100	1,980
Guatemala	900	1,455
Honduras	590	890

*1997 data   **1999 data

Source: U.S. Bureau of the Census, 1992b, 454; Population Reference Bureau, 1992; U.S. Department of State, Bureau of Inter-American Affairs, March 1998; Selig Center for Economic Growth, University of Georgia, "Hispanic Buying Power by Place of Residence 1990-1999," Nov.-Dec. 1998

much of the general population, many U.S. Hispanics are "handy" and prefer to fix their own cars and repair their own dwellings. Cultural Access Group's research has consistently shown that regardless of the type of job, a great number of Hispanics work long hours and are willing to sacrifice family and social life in order to succeed in the United States. Thus, the notion of Hispanics as lazy or lacking ambition is a wild generalization that bears no resemblance to reality. Hispanic households and families pour billions of dollars each year into the marketplace (presently estimated at over $400 billion). In fact, already a decade ago (1991), Hispanic households had over $21 billion in discretionary income (TGE Demographics, 1994). These figures alone are substantial enough to dispute the notion that aggressively marketing to Hispanics is "not worth the investment."

The fact that Hispanics earn on average less than non-Hispanic whites, and that some still live below the poverty level, should not blind marketers and other business decision-makers to the great variation in income levels and disposable income among Hispanics. As indicated in section 1, there has been a consistent and substantial increase in the income level of Hispanic households across the board, significantly reducing the number of families below the poverty level. Most important, more Hispanic households are now counted in the middle to upper income brackets. In some regions, Hispanic household income is higher than that of non-Hispanic whites. For example, a 1993 article in the *San Francisco Examiner* reports, "In well over half of all counties in California, minorities have higher average incomes than whites."

Stereotype 2: Hispanics do not wish to participate in American society.

Again, contrary to popular belief, Hispanics are becoming more and more entrenched in American society. Their participation is reflected in the growing number of Hispanic associations, libraries, research centers, and businesses throughout the United States. Furthermore, Hispanics are increasingly active in government at the federal, state, county, and city levels. They have also made significant contributions to American art, theater, literature, film, music and sports. Many studies indicate that Hispanics are willing to be part of "the American way of life." When Yankelovich's Hispanic Monitor, a longitudinal survey study that tracks Hispanic values and beliefs, asked a representative sample of U.S. Hispanics to respond to the statement, "Hispanic immigrants to the U.S. should be prepared to adapt to the American way of life," 73 percent agreed with the statement (Braus, 1993). The dramatic growth of Hispanic voters, and Hispanic-owned businesses also suggests that Hispanics are participating in American society at all levels.

Stereotype 3: *Hispanics do not acculturate.*

Hispanic consumers are acculturating into mainstream American culture, slowly, but steadily. This is particularly so among U.S.-born teens and younger adults. However, as discussed previously, the rate of acculturation of immigrant groups into the dominant society is influenced by many factors. There are a number of reasons why many Hispanics preserve their cultural values and traditions for long periods of time. The most salient one is the ongoing rate of migration of Hispanics to the United States, replenishing and reinforcing the culture on a continuing basis. In addition, relative to other immigrant groups, most Hispanics in the United States are a short distance away from their countries of origin. Proximity, freedom to cross borders, air travel, and modern means of communication facilitate contact with families and relatives back home. It is not unusual for Hispanics in the United States to travel to their country of origin during the Christmas holidays or the South American summer. Mexicans and Puerto Ricans have been traveling between the United States and their homelands for centuries. Presently, Cubans and some Central Americans are an exception, because their freedom to return to their home countries may be hindered by political restrictions in those countries.

Hispanic media also contribute to strengthening the cultural bond by keeping the Spanish language alive, and

Proximity, freedom to cross borders, air travel, and modern communications facilitate contact with families and relatives back home.

keeping all generations of U.S. Hispanics abreast of the political and social developments in their Latin-American homelands, and in the U.S. Hispanic community.

Among first-generation Hispanics, there may also be a desire to retain the Hispanic culture and language as much as possible within the family in order to return to their homeland when political or economic stability permits. Many Hispanics often come to the United States "planning" to work for several years to save enough money to make a difference to their families back home to whom they later return. For example, many native Mexicans who have lived in the United States for a long time have never bought a home here because they are always thinking about returning to *Mexico Lindo* (Beautiful Mexico).

Another factor slowing the rate of acculturation is the fact that the majority of the U.S. Hispanic adult population immigrated to the U.S. as adults; hence, their formative years took place in a Hispanic country and society. Their mind-set, values and attitudes are often difficult to change, and for many of them, learning a second language is extremely difficult. Obviously this will change with subsequent generations.

All of these elements reinforce cultural and family ties and impinge on the urgency to settle down and blend in culturally with the dominant American society. One fact to remember, however, is that most immigrants undergo some type of acculturation whether they are motivated to do so or not.

THINKING AND COMMUNICATING IN A DIFFERENT CULTURE

Understanding and thinking in a different culture is a challenge, but not impossible. Certainly, the first step is curiosity and an unbiased attitude. One must be open to learning where the cultural differences lie and how these impact your specific product or service. Building a

Many native Mexicans who have lived in the U.S. for a long time have never bought a home here because they are always thinking about returning to "Mexico Lindo."

cultural base will give you the basic tools to identify the key cultural issues. You can then manage these elements to develop and implement successful strategies and programs. The following chapters describe how to build a U.S. Hispanic cultural base.

YOU, *TU* AND *USTED*

As mentioned earlier, a practical way to understand someone from another culture is to be aware and learn to recognize the ways in which their culture and yours differ. You may have noticed, for example, differences in greeting protocols between Hispanics and Anglo-Americans. Americans have a tendency to be more informal but reserved in their initial contacts and relationships in general. Traditional Hispanics, on the other hand, tend to be more formal on first encounters and to address people by their last names, e.g., "Señor y Señora Gutierrez" (Mr. and Mrs. Gutierrez).

Similarly, in relationships, Hispanics tend to share more about their personal lives, and more often talk about their family, children, and husbands, whereas Anglo Saxons tend to be reserved regarding their personal lives.

Having said that, it must be noted that the formal versus informal social orientation varies within the U.S. Hispanic market. For example, Caribbean Latinos (Puerto Ricans, Cubans) tend to be more informal than Mexicans and Central/South Americans, particularly the younger generations.

In language, there are also linguistic and grammatical differences that impact how Latinos communicate. The English pronoun you, for example, is neutral with respect to familiarity and social position. It can be used to address a friend, a child, or the president of the United States. Such neutrality is absent from the Spanish language, where the pronoun *tu* conveys infor-

Traditional Hispanics tend to be more formal on first encounters and to address people by their titles and last names.

mality and the pronoun *usted* is formal and suggests respect and distance. It would be unthinkable for Hispanics to make use of *el tuteo*, the act of using *tu*, when addressing a public figure, or in a formal business relation. The exception is Latinos from Colombia who use *tu* and *usted* in a different way, sometimes reversing the formal with the informal pronoun use. Younger and acculturated Latinos today tend to favor using *tu* in all social interactions. For example, Generation Ñ and New Latinas rarely use *usted* especially if they are of Caribbean origin.

In sum, deciding when to use *tu* or *usted* in marketing communications is not simple and needs an insightful, knowledgeable and creative mind to decide what is the right choice. With a growing acculturating Latino market, this issue will remain a challenge that needs to be addressed—and researched—on a case-by-case basis. This is even more true if the purpose is to implement a national media campaign.

Chapter 8

How to Communicate In-Culture

Issues of language, tradition, and degree of acculturation or assimilation are of particular relevance when
addressing recently immigrated consumers. A Puerto
Rican from New York, a Cuban from Miami, and a Mexican
from San Jose, California, may read and interpret a message quite differently depending on his or her own
background. In other words, build a general knowledge
base about the overall culture of the group being targeted by becoming familiar with the everyday (micro)
aspects as well as the larger (macro) aspects of their culture (Lappin, 1983). This may sound overwhelming at
first, but you will find that there are only a few basic
issues, many of which are obvious (e.g., if somebody just
moved to a new country, chances are they have to learn
everything about America's marketplace, from the basics
to the more complex aspects of society).

*Imagine yourself in a
country where the
culture, language, and
even the alphabet are
different from your own.*

PLAY THE ROLE OF THE CONSUMER

Another helpful technique is for marketers or advertisers to take an imaginary trip to another country where
the culture, language, and even the alphabet are different from their own. Imagine yourself trying to catch a
cab in the streets of Japan or France. Picture yourself
looking for a job there and trying to learn Japanese or

Continues on page 82

Checking Your Cultural Base

How can you avoid making major blunders in advertising communications and marketing to Hispanics? The only safe way is to get close to the Hispanic consumer. Here is a checklist for getting started:

Start from scratch

> Gather as much background information as possible on the sociocultural aspects of the group you are targeting. Some Hispanics have lived in the United States for many generations, others for a few years, and still others are recent arrivals.

Become knowledgeable about your target audience's socio-psychographic background

> Places of origin, social class, income status, gender roles and age are critical to the success of interethnic communications.

Learn about people's relationship to your product or service

> Never assume you can simply translate your general market market effort to an immigrant market segment. If the target group is primarily foreign-born, learn how they lived at home. Did they use the product or service you are promoting, say a checking or savings account? Or did they have credit cards before immigrating? Credit cards are available everywhere in the world, but they are not as pervasive as they are in the United States. You need to learn if your target consumers have experience or are familiar with the product or service you are promoting. Did these consumers have a telephone at home in their native towns? If not, why not? Did they

have microwaves or refrigerators? How about insurance? Did they know anyone who had home insurance? If not, you must start your marketing campaign from an introductory strategy. The same logic and process needs to be used with every product or service category.

Pay attention to the specifics

Forms of interaction, such as body language, tone of voice and expressions carry great emotional value in face-to-face communications. They must be "in-culture," that is, in the culture of the specific consumer group.

Be aware of differences

Make a point of finding out the dos and don'ts of the targeted culture's society. Learn about the culture of each target segment as described earlier in this section. For example, when addressing Hispanic adults, you should refer to them as Mr. or Mrs. and avoid using first names unless you consider yourself a personal friend of the family.

Learn About Their Accomplishments

Become familiar with the contributions Hispanics have made to American culture, business, politics, the military, and other areas that you can use in your advertising and marketing endeavors.

French. Imagine looking for a pharmacy to buy medicine for your sick child or trying to locate a hospital in case of an emergency. Simply visualize yourself shopping in a store or supermarket—trying to find a product with no one available to help you. Chances are you would feel miserable, inadequate, and ill-prepared in the new environment. Suddenly, all your survival skills accumulated over the course of a lifetime fall flat in the new surroundings and you feel the need for a helping hand. The pressure and the stress can be overwhelming, but you must go on.

Under these circumstances, wouldn't you welcome an 800 number that you could call for basic information and hear a friendly English-speaking operator respond to your questions? Wouldn't you favor signs reading "We Speak English" or "Welcome"? Wouldn't you feel comforted if there was a friend or a familiar face to give you a helping hand while you learned the ways of the new country?

Although marketers and advertising agents are not substitutes for family or friends, they do play an important role in assisting U.S. immigrant populations with some of their needs. By advertising in Spanish, providing 800 numbers, and giving Hispanic consumers useful information about the availability and benefits of their products and services, not only are you promoting your business, but also helping immigrant consumers adapt to American society.

To effectively communicate with the Hispanic market and gain share of heart, you need to get to know Hispanic consumers by learning as much as possible about who they are, how they live, their likes and dislikes and what they enjoy in life. Recognizing and dealing with stereotypes is the starting point. Coming to terms with personal biases provides the framework for an image change, ensuring that the company approaches Hispanic consumers with a "business mind" and not from a "human resources" perspective. This will also help ensure brands and services are viewed favorably by the Hispanic market.

Visiting Hispanic Households

To learn about current or potential customers, you should do more than read a few books. You should gain firsthand experience with the target audience and take the time to tour, in this case, Hispanic neighborhoods, stores, restaurants, and movie theaters, and attend Hispanic cultural events. It would be extremely valuable to be a guest in a Mexican, Puerto Rican, Cuban, or Salvadoran household—to sit down with the family, eat what they eat, and share their experiences. Travel and vacation in Latin America. If this is not feasible, try Hispanic-specific trade show seminars and cultural crash-courses. In other words, go out into the community: "Taste the soup to know the soup" (Minuchin, 1981).

One of the Cultural Access Group's most successful seminar and trade show presentations is a slide show portraying Hispanic families. The visuals capture Hispanics of different regions, acculturation levels, countries of origin, legal status and socioeconomic status. The slides include pictures of U.S. Hispanic homes, including kitchens, dining rooms, bathrooms, gardens, and garages. One reason for the great appeal of this show, "Visiting Hispanic Households" (1986), is that it opens a window for the audience to see what Hispanic consumers are really like. The vignettes offer viewers a "reality check," allowing them to confront their preconceptions and discover a different reality.

One slide takes the audience to the house of a family of "illegal aliens" to discover a neat apartment where pride is taken in well-groomed children and clean and shiny floors. Although it is a humble dwelling, the level of care, the pride of the household members, and the

confidence of the wife in providing a comfortable home are readily apparent. These slides help dispel the prevalent notion that all undocumented Hispanic immigrants live in crowded conditions.

Other photos portray more sophisticated Hispanic households, homes displaying an array of electronic goods, art, and a definite Latin taste in the decor. Again and again, seminar participants have praised the "visits" to typical Hispanic households simply because the experience allowed them to clear their minds of stereotypes and myths that limited their ability to truly see Hispanics for who and what they are. The visuals helped marketers understand the importance of the theme, "To sell me is to know me."

THE LATINO MARKET IS MANY MARKETS

Chapter 9

How to "Think" Hispanic

Ideally, someone working with consumers of a different culture would want to think and feel from the perspective of that culture. There are two very practical tools for doing this: Life Cycle comparison and the Ecosystemic model. These tools can help you visualize how cultural differences emerge and how these differences affect consumer behavior. This understanding allows you to modify strategy and approach when marketing to Hispanic consumers. Both tools were originally presented by family therapists, Drs. Celia J. Falicov and Betty M. Karrer (1986), to explain behavioral patterns and differences between "traditional Mexican-American" families living in a rural environment and "Anglo middle class" families. The constructs were intended to aid family counselors dealing with clients in the process of adapting to American society, but are very useful applied to thinking in a different cultural environment.

When targeting consumers across cultures, what is lacking is a cultural awareness. Given the complexity of the U.S. Hispanic market, how should you as a business executive, marketer, or advertiser manage the different levels of acculturation and the cultural diversity of Hispanics in the marketplace?

What is needed is a framework—a point of view—that will allow you (and your company) to approach Hispanic consumers from within their own culture, background, and socioeconomic characteristics. This frame of

Life Cycle comparison and the Ecosystemic model are tools that help business executives, marketers, and advertisers visualize how cultural differences emerge and how these differences affect consumer behavior.

reference will help you understand what it is that makes U.S. Hispanic consumers "tick," and how these consumers differ from their Anglo-American counterparts. Marketers and advertisers need an in-culture understanding to develop ads, images, and messages that communicate successfully with a Hispanic audience—messages that will captivate consumers by conveying "I know you."

Cultural sensitivity is the key to ensuring that your ads do not backfire or distract the consumer from effectively seeing or hearing your message. Suppose you are designing a television advertisement for a Hispanic audience and the commercial requires the presence of a minor or a woman. Can you show a Hispanic child playing alone and unsupervised in a nonfamily environment? Or can you show a young adult Hispanic woman living by herself? Can you show a Hispanic woman drinking an alcoholic beverage alone? A yes to any of these questions might well result in a commercial that could backfire.

Why could they backfire? Commercials designed for Hispanic viewers will frequently and mistakenly reflect the lifestyles and idiosyncrasies of Anglo-American viewers. The prevalent attitude among some advertisers is that a few adjustments here and there are all that is needed to elicit the response of a Hispanic audience. Unfortunately, these minor adjustments overlook cultural nuances and value differences. These variations may not be readily apparent to the management in a company and frequently are not detected with standardized copy testing methods or survey questionnaires. But the variations will surface if the commercials are subjected to in-depth, unstructured qualitative probing in focus groups or one-on-one interviews with representatives of the targeted Hispanic consumer group. The following tools provide ways to check how close your thinking or strategy is to that of the core Hispanic customer.

DIFFERENT LIFE STAGES

We may find ourselves entertaining thoughts such as "By now I should have finished college, or should be married, or should have children;" "I have a good executive position even though I am still young; my father got his when he was much older;" "My daughter is dating—soon she will be married, leave home, and have children; I will become a grandparent and have a house full of empty rooms." These thoughts or similar ones reflect people's life cycle-related expectations as they move through different stages in their lives.

Most of us have been unconsciously "programmed" to expect land-mark events to take place by the time we reach a certain age. These pro-grammed life-cycle landmarks are "culturally" driven and hence vary between cultures. Therefore, the various events that mark the transition from one stage to another in the life cycle should be taken into account to develop effective marketing communication and campaigns in other cultures. For each stage there is a preconceived set of expecta-tions in the viewer's mind; a commercial should match those expecta-tions. For example, the age a child begins school, the age at which traditional Hispanic families free their daughters of the presence of a chaperone, or the time that an oldest son begins caring for his elderly parents are socially determined.

The life-cycle models of traditional Mexican-American and Anglo-American families are quite different. As illustrated by the life-cycle models in **Figure 9.1** and **Figure 9.2**, relationships among traditional

FIGURE 9.1

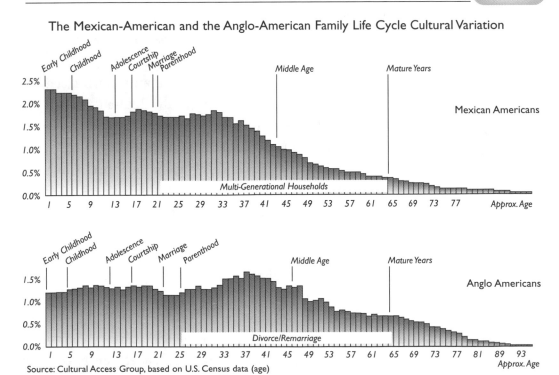

The Mexican-American and the Anglo-American Family Life Cycle Cultural Variation

Source: Cultural Access Group, based on U.S. Census data (age)

FIGURE 9.2

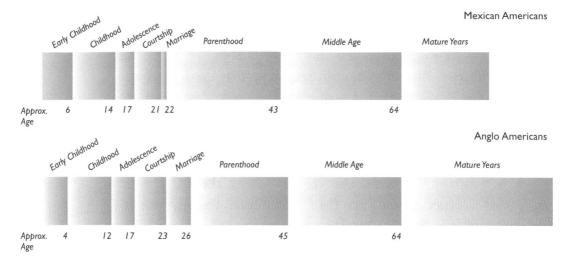

The Mexican-American and the Anglo-American Family Life Cycle Cultural Variation

Source: Cultural Access Group,, based on U.S. Census (age); Falicov and Karrer, 1986

To many Hispanics, courtship is a long and intense lifetime event.

Mexican families tend to have longer histories. While non-Hispanics tend to spend more years in the courtship phase, it is customary for young Hispanics to date the same person for a long time before marriage. Hispanic couples tend to stay married longer, and Hispanic children tend to separate from their parents much later than do most Anglo-American children, usually not until they get married. For Mexican-American families, these arrangements allow for greater parental intervention in their children's lives. In Mexican-American culture, there are fewer courtships, there is greater emphasis on romance, and the pressure for the families to know the bride or groom and their families is greater. To many Hispanics, courtship is a long and intense lifetime event. Hispanics also tend to divorce less often than non-Hispanics.

As a marketer, your familiarity with the events of the target audience life cycle will enhance your understanding of their attitudes and beliefs. Such awareness will improve your ability to select themes and timing that appeal to Hispanic sentiments. By choosing situations that fit into everyday Hispanic life, you gain the minds, hearts, and approval of your audience. For example, Hispanic families, on average, tend to send their children to school later than the general market. Hispanic mothers want to keep "baby" at home for as long as possible. Therefore, a manufacturer of toys may want to capitalize on the fact that this mother will need to keep the child entertained and busy while she takes care of the household chores without the traditional help of the extended family. This mother will welcome learning practical ways to take care of the child and the household. Many ready-to-serve foods and products may also be promoted to this particular growing market segment—the Hispanic mother in child-rearing years.

Hispanic families, on average, tend to send their children to school later than the general market.

ENVIRONMENT MAKES A DIFFERENCE

Anyone who has lived in the United States since birth is probably imbued with the values and beliefs underlying Anglo-American culture. Success, individualism, freedom, equality, competition and a strong work ethic are some of the values that are central to the American character. Compare and contrast these values with those typical of Hispanic culture—group orientation, authority, class distinction, religion, respect, faith, fate, and family loyalty. These values vary from country to country, and within a country between rural and urban centers, but in general they are common across Latin-American culture. These values are passed from one generation to the next, but may change or weaken as Hispanics integrate into mainstream American culture.

Understanding the differences in infrastructure between Latin-American countries and the United States helps explain differences between how Hispanics and Americans organize their daily lives. For example, in the United States, not having a telephone is almost unthinkable. Moreover, having to wait as long as an entire week for the telephone service to be connected sounds totally outrageous. In Latin America, getting a telephone can be an unrealistic proposition, due to a lack of telephone lines or bureaucratic red tape. A similar distinction is evident when it comes to owning a car. In places like California, where distances between home and work can be great and public transportation is limited, owning a vehicle is a matter of livelihood. By contrast, in most of Latin America, owning a car is a luxury, and public transportation is the way most people commute to their jobs.

Organizational differences between Latin and Anglo cultures exist at all levels of transportation, news, banking, health, merchandising, education and so on. Thus, business people need to be familiar with the backgrounds of Hispanics. It is surprising how different their experiences are from those of the general market.

THE ECOSYSTEMIC MODEL

Unlike the life-cycle model, which views Hispanics from the perspective of the individual in his or her relation to family, the ecosystemic model approaches consumers from the perspective of the individual and his or her relationship to society. As the name implies, the ecosystemic model looks at the individual from an ecological perspective. It considers all levels or layers of society in which we operate (**Figure 9.3**). This model

FIGURE 9.3

The Ecosystemic Model

The model shows the different levels of societal interaction, no matter what the culture.

Macrosystem: Addresses general relationships with prototypes of ideas of the culture or subculture (ideology and myths) that set patterns for the interactions that occur at the concrete level

Exosystem: Addresses interactions with major institutions in society such as government, church, and media

Mesosystem: Addresses inter-relationships with major institutions or settings such as extended family, workplace, school peer group, and neighborhood

Microsystem: Addresses relationships within the family

Source: M. Isabel Valdéz, 1991; Bronfenbrenner, U. & Falicov, C. J., 1977

is a tool that allows one to examine how individuals from different cultures interact between, and within, the different layers of society and shows where there is room for "dissonance." Dissonance means that when the forms of interaction in a particular social layer of one culture are different from those of another culture, the doors are open to confusion, frustration, and misinterpretation. The model helps explain areas in which Hispanics are changing and adopting to different forms of interaction with their new society.

As previously mentioned, psychologists Falicov and Karrer adapted the ecosystemic model from one by Urie Bronfenbenner (1977) to help explain the cultural and social difficulties immigrants encounter when moving to the United States. Even though the model was designed to represent Mexican working-class people, the author has successfully applied it to explain and uncover behavioral traits of Hispanics from other countries and socioeconomic groups. The model is described with a diagram representing traditional working-class Mexican-Americans and modern middle-class Anglo-Americans.

FIGURE 9.4

The Ecosystemic Model

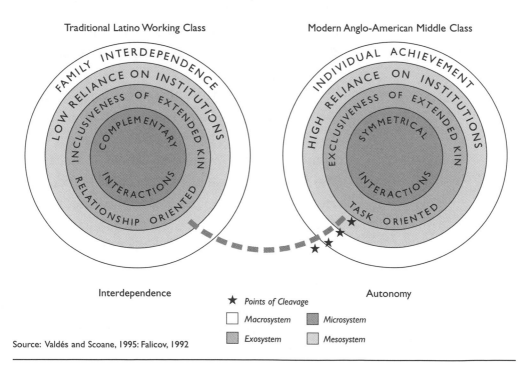

Source: Valdés and Scoane, 1995: Falicov, 1992

Relative to Anglo Americans, Hispanics tend to have fewer checking accounts, make less use of financial institutions, and have fewer real estate loans.

The ecosystemic model (**Figure 9.4**) places the individual at the center of the circle (the microsystem). This first circle represents the individual's interactions at the core of the family. Whereas the individual in the Anglo model tends to make decisions unilaterally, the Latino will try to make his or her decisions complement the needs of the family group.

The next layer (the mesosystem) explains how individuals interact in the work place, neighborhood, school, peer group, or extended family. Whereas Anglos tend to be task-oriented, Latinos will focus on the relationships.

The next layer (the exosystem) includes the institutions that organize everyone's lives—government, business, banks, utilities, and media. Anglos tend to have a high reliance on these institutions, whereas Latinos rely on them less.

Finally, the outside layer (the macrosystem) refers to the larger, broader, intangible layer where there are shared values, beliefs, attitudes norms, and aspirations common to people sharing a distinct culture (Falicov and Karrer, 1986). For Anglos, individual achievement rules. For Latinos, family interdependence takes precedence.

Within each culture, there is usually consonance (tacit agreement) between the values that are practiced and the ones the culture believes in. However, between cultures (e.g., the Anglo and Latino), dissonance can arise because the values of the cultures differ. As you can see in Figure 9.4, there is potential for dissonance in virtually every layer of these two cultures, but thinking about the differences helps the marketer to identify where that dissonance may occur.

How does the Ecosystemic model work? Think of the many Hispanic immigrants who will arrive in the United States during the next ten years. Think about the Hispanic immigrants who are already here. Have you ever wondered why so many make purchases on a cash basis and do not have checking accounts? Relative to Anglo Americans, Hispanics tend to have fewer checking accounts, make less use of financial institutions, and have fewer real estate loans.

The Ecosystemic model provides a framework for dealing with these types of issues. It shows how traditional working-class Latinos relate to institutions vis-á-vis middle-class Anglo Americans. Hispanics tend to rely less on institutions than do middle-class Anglo Americans. Lack of trust in institutions is a common trait among many Latin Americans.

Origin of the
American dollar sign ($)

Why should Hispanics rely less on institutions such as government and banks? Years of unstable currencies, high inflation, frequent devaluations, and even political instability in their native countries have engendered a "no-trust" attitude toward banks, institutions, and most forms of government. Why put money away that will be worthless tomorrow? Better to spend it on tangible items such as jewelry, appliances, and furniture than to have it evaporate from the bank's coffers. In most Latin-American countries, currency changes denominations frequently. In Argentina during the late 1980s and early 1990s, for example, inflation reached heights of more than 3,000 percent. In Argentina, as well as in many other Latin-American countries, devaluation ate up savings so fast that parents would not think of opening a savings account at the birth of a child, because they would be likely to have nothing to show for it by the child's 18th birthday.

Years of unstable currencies, high inflation, frequent devaluations, and even political instability in their native countries have engendered a "no-trust" attitude toward banks, institutions, and most forms of government among many Latin Americans.

In addition to a dearth of trust, a substantial number of people in Latin America have never had familiarity with or access to a bank. Checking accounts are common among the wealthy, the upper-middle class, businesses, and corporations. Unlike banking practices

In the Hispanic model, it is expected that the parents provide for the children until they are young adults, continuing the tradition of long-term family interdependency.

in the United States, where the requirements are minimal and opening a checking account takes a matter of minutes, banking practices in most Latin-American countries are strict and opening a checking account may take months. Therefore, it is not unusual for Latin Americans to conduct their transactions in cash all the time. In the non-affluent classes, it is normal to buy a house and pay for it in cash, borrowing the funds from friends or relatives, if necessary. Because Latin-American consumers deal primarily in cash, their knowledge of how banks function is very limited, and they bring this lack of familiarity with them when they move to the United States. This prevents many recently arrived Latin immigrants from making initial contact with banks.

Any business seeking to attract Hispanic consumers should take into account the consumers' previous experience with that type of institution, service, or product.

Another example using the ecosystemic model can be observed at the family level. The usual forms of interaction inside the Hispanic family tend to be different than those at the heart of the American middle class. Hispanics tend to stress interdependence within the family whereas Americans tend to stress autonomy (see **Figure 9.4**). This affects, for example, how children in both cultures obtain cash to buy things they like.

In the American family, it would be perfectly acceptable for the child to find a job and earn his or her money for personal use or savings. It is actually encouraged. American children can be seen delivering newspapers, selling lemonade or cookies, and engaging in other methods of earning spending money. These activities would be unthinkable for nonacculturated, traditional Hispanic families where a child is encouraged to earn money only when the family is under severe financial stress. In the Hispanic model, it is expected that the parents provide for the children until they are young adults, continuing the tradition of long-term family interdependency. Similarly, the Hispanic mother will be responsible for the child's weekly laundry and food preparation until he or she is a young adult.

Family interdependency can help explain why some Hispanic mothers continue cooking for their adult children, why Hispanics tend to stick together on weekends, and why parents tend to encourage their children to stay with them for as long as possible. It is within this context that the ecosystemic model becomes valuable to marketers, advertisers, businesses, or any organization attempting to unravel the social differences that exist between Hispanics and Anglo-Americans. The ecosystemic model lends a hand to grasp the ongoing acculturation process Hispanics and others start to go through from the moment they arrive in the United States.

Certainly many of these traits change with acculturation, and there is pressure to function in a society where the extended family is not present and, unlike Latin America, affordable domestic help is hard to find. These behaviors and forms of interaction must be taken into consideration when marketing to nonacculturated Hispanics and should be recognized and used in the creative development process.

Chapter 10

¿What's in a Name?
Cultural Diversity within the Market

What is the difference between *fruta bomba* and *papaya*? None. Both terms refer to the same tropical fruit. But to western Cubans, the word *papaya* is taboo because it also refers to a part of the female anatomy, whereas for the rest of Latin Americans, it is just a fruit. Both Mexicans and Spaniards eat *tortillas*. But the Mexican *tortilla* is a corn cake, whereas the Spanish *tortilla* is a cousin of the omelette. Mexicans and Mexican Americans eat *tortas* as part of the main course, but Chileans, Argentines, and Peruvians have them as dessert. *Torta* is a sandwich and sometimes a cheeseless omelette for Mexicans, but is a sweet cake for the other two groups.

Beans are a very important staple in the Caribbean, Mexico, Central America, and South America. But each country may refer to them and cook them quite differently. Puerto Ricans refer to beans as *habichuelas* and Mexicans call them *frijoles*. Nicaraguans like to eat *gallo pinto* (rice and beans), Puerto Ricans eat *arroz con gandules* (rice and beans), Cubans eat Christians and Moors (beans with rice), and Spaniards eat *paella* (a rice dish). Chileans and others in the southern zone call beans *porotos* and prepare them as a soup dish.

To get to the restaurant Cubans and Puerto Ricans ride the *gua-gua*, Mexicans the *camion*, Chileans the *micro,* Peruvians the bus, and Argentines the omnibus. The fact is, each group travels by bus. Peruvians, Argentines, and Spaniards drive *coches* (cars), Mexicans, Cubans, and Venezuelans drive their *carros* (cars), and still other nationalities drive the *automovil.*

These examples illustrate some cultural variations found among Hispanics from different countries. They also tend to differ from one another in the sports they favor, the music they listen to, the art they produce, and the theater they prefer.

The list that follows is a compilation of attributes that differ among the three major U.S. Hispanic groups: Mexicans, Cubans, and Puerto Ricans. Although comprehensive, the list is by no means exhaustive.

It must be kept in mind that some of the differences listed are merely tendencies—directional, not cast in iron. This list includes characteristics that reflect historical patterns, cultural affinity and diversity, immigration patterns, self-identification, social relationships with other Hispanics and with Anglos, socioeconomic differences, and differences in health habits and religion.

Fortunately, there are similarities enough among Latino sub-groups to make it possible to find a cultural common denominator to create a national campaign that talks to all Latinos independent of their countries of origin.

Puerto Ricans refer to beans as habichuelas, and Mexicans call them frijoles.

U.S. MEXICANS

SIZE AND LOCATION

The largest of all U.S. Hispanic groups.

The majority reside in the southwestern United States (California, Colorado, Arizona, New Mexico, Texas). There are growing Mexican populations in Chicago, Illinois, and Miami, Florida.

PRESENCE IN THE UNITED STATES

Except for the colonial Spaniards, the Mexican presence in what is today the United States precedes that of other Hispanic groups. Mexicans were present in California, Texas, Arizona, and New Mexico prior to American independence. By about 1850, the Mexican population in New Mexico alone was approximately 60,000, according to some sources (Kanellos, 1993).

IMMIGRATION-RELATED EVENTS

Labor migration to the United States precedes that of Puerto Ricans, Cubans and other Hispanic groups. Mexicans have greater restrictions on immigrating to the United States than the other two groups.

American immigration initiatives to attract low-wage earners, such as the Bracero Program, enticed Mexicans to join the U.S. labor force in 1942.

Motivation to migrate: poor economic conditions in Mexico, desire to improve standard of living, and family reunification (National Association of Latino Appointed Officials, 1992).

Larger undocumented immigration than Puerto Ricans and Cubans.

CULTURAL INFLUENCES

Aztec civilization, Spain, Mexico, and the United States.

Indigenous influence greater than in Puerto Rico.

LANGUAGE

Mexican Spanish influenced by American indigenous elements, for example, *tomate, aguacate, chocolate, chile.* Most of the borrowing refers to flora, fauna, and rustic instruments found in rural Mexico.

Mexican Spanish tends to pronounce all the consonants (unlike Caribbean Spanish, where the final consonants are "swallowed").

Some of the most prevalent indigenous words found among Mexicans and Mexican Americans are *zacate* (grass, lawn), *elote* (corn), *papalote* (toy kite), *quajolote* (turkey), and *tecolote* (owl), *cacahuate* (peanuts).

SELF-IDENTIFICATION

U.S. Mexicans identify themselves as Mexican, Latino, Mexican American, Chicano, and La Raza.

Strong identification with Mexican cultural heritage.

Weak identification with other Hispanic groups.

Limited contact with individuals from other Hispanic groups.

Tendency to think of themselves as being somewhat similar "culturally" and "politically" to other Latinos.

More likely than other Hispanic groups to report discrimination in the United States (de la Garza, 1992).

Report having positive relations with Anglos (de la Garza, 1992).

U.S. Mexicans

SOCIOECONOMIC CHARACTERISTICS

Higher household income than Puerto Ricans but lower than Cubans, Central and South Americans, and other Hispanic groups in the United States.

Younger than Puerto Ricans, Cubans, and other Hispanics.

Larger households than Cubans or Puerto Ricans.

More U.S. Mexicans own their homes than do Puerto Ricans and Central and South Americans, but homeownership is most prevalent among Cubans and other Hispanic groups.

VALUES

Strong family values prevail. Family ideology requires individual sacrifice for the good of the family. Mexicans are more group-oriented than other Hispanic groups.

They have the largest families of all U.S. Hispanic groups.

Extended families (residing with relatives) are more prevalent among immigrants.

Recent immigrants tend to rely more on family kinship and social networks than U.S.-born Mexican Americans.

There is a tendency to intermarry. Women of Mexican origin are more likely than men to marry non-Hispanics.

Divorce is less socially acceptable among U.S. Mexicans than U.S. Puerto Ricans, Cubans, and Central and South Americans (Kanellos, 1983; U.S. Bureau of the Census, 1992b).

POLITICAL ISSUES

Mexicans are more active politically and have the greatest Hispanic political representation in U.S. society.

Cubans follow. They defend cultural heritage, equal rights and bilingual education.

HEALTH

U.S. Mexicans tend to seek medical care less often and postpone doing so more often than other ethnic groups.

U.S. Mexicans appear to rely heavily on vitamins, mineral supplements and medicinal herbs.

U.S. Mexican children (aged 5 and under) have lower exposure to cigarette smoking (40 percent) before and after birth than all other Hispanics (44 percent) and non-Hispanics (51 percent).

U.S. Mexicans are less open than any other Hispanic group to discussing sexually transmitted diseases. For example, Mexican-American parents are much less likely to have ever discussed AIDS with their children (50 percent) than mainland Puerto Ricans (74 percent) or other Hispanic adults (64 percent) (Biddlecom and Hardy, 1991; Overpeck and Moss, 1991; U.S. Bureau of the Census, 1992b).

RELIGION

Most U.S. Mexicans are Catholic.

Fewer Mexicans than other Hispanic groups are Protestant.

A growing number of Mexican Americans are Pentecostals.

Spiritual practices: European Spiritualism is the practice of evoking the spirit of the dead through mediums; it is considered a pseudoscience.

Spiritualism is a cult that developed in Mexico among practicing Catholics. Spiritualists act as agents for great religious figures for the purpose of healing. It is also present in other parts of South America.

U.S. Mexicans

Other practices involve *yerberias* (specialty stores selling medicinal herbs and plants) and the *yerbero* (an herb specialist knowledgeable about the medicinal qualities of plants). *Curanderismo* is the practice of healing by invoking the forces of good and evil.

ART

U.S. Mexican art is strongly influenced by Catholicism and the sociocultural experience of Mexicans in the United States. The following types of art are prevalent:

Religious Art

Religious art is common in the southwestern United States (New Mexico, Texas, Arizona). It focuses essentially on religious themes such as the Virgin de Guadalupe, *santos* (saints) churches and altars. Modern religious art originated as a response to a popular demand for private oratories, altars, and shrines. As such, religious art is usually conceived, produced, and marketed by families rather than single artists.

Mexican-American Art

Mexican-American art was part of mainstream American art from about 1920 to 1950. Unlike religious art, Mexican-American art draws essentially on American and Hispanic regional themes. During the 1960s, murals, one of the main modes of expressions of Mexican-American art, took various forms: figurative, abstract, pop-funk, and destructive.

Chicano Art Movement

Prominent in California, Texas, New Mexico, and the Great Lakes region, Chicano art focuses on pre-Columbian, Mexican and Chicano motifs and themes depicting historically controversial relations between

Anglos and Mexicans. Popular themes include politics, feminism, *barrio* life, street life, farm-worker communities, Chicano culture and identity, and religion. Art media include murals, sculpture, drawings, silk screens, photography, graphics, and ceramics. Since the 1970s, Chicano painters, printmakers, sculptors, and poster artists have increasingly displayed their work in local and regional events and major exhibitions.

Chicano Murals

Contemporary mural painting became popular in the 1970s. Muralists use walls of housing projects, alleys, concrete stairways, grocery stores, pharmacies, and cultural centers in Mexican communities. Many of the murals address social concerns.

MUSIC

U.S.-Mexican music, prevalent in Texas, New Mexico, Arizona, and California, is unique for its cultural context and Mexican heritage. Partly for this reason it is much less eclectic than musical forms found among other U.S. Hispanic groups. U.S.-Mexican music has been less influenced than other groups by African culture and the type of instrumentation found in the music played by Caribbean Hispanics. The following types are commonly recognized:

Música Norteña

Also known as the *conjunto, música norteña* was developed by Mexican Texans as a vocal expression of intercultural conflict between the U.S.-Mexican working-class and Anglo establishment as well as between the Mexican working-class and more acculturated, upwardly mobile Mexican Americans. This type of music has deep cultural roots.

U.S.
Mexicans

Orquesta Tejana

Orquesta tejana is an orchestral musical form of the music preferred by acculturated, upwardly mobile Mexican Americans.

Grupos cumbieros, or tropicales modernos

A variant of *música tropical/moderna* (or Afro-Caribbean music), *grupos cumbieros* originated with Mexican immigrants in the United States during the 1960s (Kanellos, 1993).

There is a revival of Latin-American music to which first- and second-generation Hispanic artists are contributing. There is a crossover from a strictly Spanish-speaking to a broad English-speaking audience. Cubans have been instrumental in revitalizing Latin jazz, which has great appeal to second-generation Hispanics who speak English and understand Spanish. This new trend has triggered music mail clubs, such as the Club Musica Latina, that offer ready access to current and classical Hispanic music (Holston, 1992).

An example of this revival is the success of band music and *guebradita* (music and dance). Both are very popular in California and the southwest. These rhythms have emerged as new expressions of popular Mexican music from different provinces.

LITERATURE

Massive production in English and Spanish. Major emphasis on Mexican heritage and Anglo-Mexican conflicts.

Leads all other U.S. Hispanic groups in literary production.

Mexican heritage is rich in poetry, drama, the novel, autobiographies; also *corridos* (ballads) and short stories.

THEATER

The U.S.-Mexican theater, another cultural expression of the Mexican working class in the United States, employs Spanish or Spanish and English, has a rural orientation, and a strong pre-Columbian heritage. It portrays social issues affecting Chicanos in the United States, such as life among farm workers, Vietnam War participation, bilingual education, community control, and drugs.

El Teatro Campesino is a popular Mexican-American theater group that emerged as a support group during the farm workers' strike in California during the 1970s.

SPORTS

Soccer, boxing, and equestrian sports—horse racing, bullriding, and rodeo.

FOOD

Mexican-Indian, Native American, and Spanish influences.

U.S. PUERTO RICANS

SIZE AND LOCATION

Puerto Ricans are the second-largest Hispanic group in the United States.

Most mainland U.S. Puerto Ricans live on the East Coast (New York, New Jersey, and Florida).

LEGAL STATUS

Puerto Ricans are U.S. citizens and move freely in and out of the commonwealth.

MIGRATION

Economic considerations and family reunions are the main reasons for frequent travel between the United States and the island of Puerto Rico.

In 1944, the government program Operation Bootstrap was designed to stimulate industrialization on the island and to fill a U.S. labor shortage. It stimulated a major wave of worker migration to the United States.

DOMINANT CULTURAL INFLUENCES

Afro-Antillana (Caribbean, French), Spanish, and Anglo.

The Puerto Rican indigenous culture was wiped out by disease in the 1580s and was replaced by African slaves.

LANGUAGE

Puerto Ricans share language elements of Caribbean Spanish with Cubans and Dominicans (see "Language" section in discussion of U.S. Cubans).

There is a tendency among Puerto Ricans to pronounce the "rr" sound as "h," as in ham. The tendency is rather prevalent among Puerto Ricans from rural regions and has become a symbol of cultural identification.

The replacement of "r" by "l" at the end of words or after consonants is also prevalent, *trabajar* (work) becomes *trabajal*.

SELF-IDENTIFICATION

Puerto Ricans (Nuevo Ricans) and "Nuyoricans" (Puerto Ricans born in New York).

Strong identification with other Puerto Ricans even among U.S.-born generations.

Lower identification with other Hispanic groups and with Anglos. As with Cubans and Mexicans, Puerto Ricans tend to socialize among themselves.

Feelings of discrimination among Puerto Ricans tend to be lower than among Mexicans, but higher than among Cubans.

SOCIOECONOMIC CHARACTERISTICS

On average, the lowest socioeconomic status among all Hispanic groups.

Older than U.S. Mexicans but younger than other Hispanic groups.

Smaller households than U.S.-Mexicans and Central and South Americans, but larger than U.S. Cubans.

Puerto Rican homeownership is the lowest among all Hispanic groups (U.S. Bureau of the Census, 1991a; Schick and Schick, 1991).

VALUES

Strong family ideology and reliance on the extended family.

U.S. Puerto Ricans

Patriarch still important but decreasingly so, as more Puerto Rican women head households and join the labor force. Matriarchy present in some groups. Nuclear family formation continues to be preferred.

Most Puerto Ricans tend to feel ambivalent regarding Puerto Rico's sociopolitical relationship with the United States.

Have smaller average families (3.5 members) than U.S.-Mexicans (4 members) but larger than U.S.-Cubans (3.2 members). More variation in family types than in other Hispanic groups. Divorce is more socially accepted. Puerto Ricans have the second highest divorce rate (8.9 percent) of Hispanic subgroups.

POLITICAL ISSUES

Increased political power in United States.

Independence and statehood movements on island of Puerto Rico.

HEALTH

Medicinal herbs and home remedies are usual practices.

Have a higher consumption of vitamin and mineral products than U.S. Cubans or Mexicans.

Puerto Ricans tend to be more open about discussing AIDS with their children than are Mexicans or other Hispanic adults (Biddlecom and Hardy, 1991; U.S. Bureau of the Census, 1992b).

RELIGION

Mostly Catholic.

Non-Christian cults, including *santeria*. (See "Religion" section under discussion of U.S. Cubans).

MUSIC

See "Music" section under discussion of U.S. Cubans.

LITERATURE

U.S.-Puerto Rican literature is more recent and less abundant in general. Notable poetry and drama.

Written primarily in English (Augenbraum and Stavans, 1993).

THEATER

Nuyorican Theater began with Puerto Rican artists born in New York. It includes collectively created street theater and works by individual playwrights. Major plays are associated with Puerto Rican working-class culture. The term "Nuyorican" has not always been well received by Puerto Rican artists themselves (Kanellos, 1993).

SPORTS

Baseball.

FOOD

African and Spanish influence; tropical cuisine.

U.S. CUBANS

SIZE AND LOCATION

Third-largest Hispanic group in the United States.

Largely concentrated in the state of Florida.

PRESENCE IN THE UNITED STATES

During Cuba's first attempt at independence from Spain (1868), a large number of Cubans left for the United States and Europe.

In 1898 Spain and the United States signed the Treaty of Paris, and Spain ceded Cuba and Puerto Rico to the United States.

In 1901 under the Platt Amendment, Cuba was made a protectorate of the United States.

In 1934 Cuban sovereignty is unrestricted after United States abrogation of the Platt Amendment.

In 1959 Fidel Castro ousted Fulgencio Batista as leader of Cuba and declared Cuba a Communist state (1961), resulting in a "closed" U.S.-Cuban border.

In 1980 a brief wave of immigrants arrived in the Mariel boatlift. They were called the *Marielitos*.

In 1994 fleeing the severe deterioration of the economic conditions of Cuba, *Balceros* people used rafts to cross the Florida straits and migrated to the United States.

LEGAL STATUS

Cuban immigrants have political refugee status.

Unlike Puerto Ricans, Cubans cannot commute freely between the United States and their homeland and are not U.S. citizens, unless they have been naturalized or were born in the U.S.

MIGRATION

Historically, political and economic instability has been the main factor in Cuban-U.S. migration.

Travel restrictions exist between the United States and Cuba.

DOMINANT CULTURAL INFLUENCES

Spain and Africa, some Chinese and French.

LANGUAGE

Pronunciation is the most salient difference between Caribbean Spanish and Mexican Spanish. There is a habit among Cubans, Puerto Ricans, and Dominicans to omit the final consonants. Reportedly, the "swallowing" of consonants contributes to the popular impression that Spanish Caribbean is spoken faster than other forms of Spanish.

Cubans prefer the diminutive *ico* as opposed to the Spanish *ito* as in *momentico, chiquitico,* and so on. (Kanellos, 1993).

SELF-IDENTIFICATION

U.S. Cubans identify themselves primarily with their national origin and only somewhat with other Hispanic groups. They rarely mingle with individuals from other Hispanic groups. Cubans are more likely than Mexicans or Puerto Ricans to think of themselves as being different from Latinos.

Cubans report feeling less discriminated against than Mexicans or Puerto Ricans and report having closer relations to Anglos than to other Hispanic groups in general.

U.S. Cubans

Cubans in New York are perceived by Dominicans and Colombians as the most prejudiced group among Latinos.

SOCIOECONOMIC CHARACTERISTICS

U.S. Cubans tend to be older and wealthier. In proportion, more of them are professionals, and they have more years of schooling than any other Hispanic group except for South Americans. Recent immigration waves (1980 *Marielitos* and 1994 *Balceros*) are changing this socioeconomic profile.

U.S. Cuban households are smaller than any other Hispanic group and smaller than those of white non-Hispanics.

In the United States, more Cubans own their homes than do Mexicans and other Hispanics, (Schick and Schick, 1991; U.S. Bureau of the Census, 1993c).

VALUES

Strong family ideology, kinship, and social network. Favor paternalism within the nuclear family.

Value system closer to American than any other Hispanic group. Favor individualism and upward mobility.

U.S. Cubans have smaller families than Mexicans or Puerto Ricans.

U.S. Cubans tend to marry within the group, but among those who do not, Cuban men tend to marry non-Hispanics more than do Cuban, Mexican, and Puerto Rican women, but less than do Central and South Americans and other Hispanic women.

Divorce is socially acceptable among U.S. Cubans (and in Cuba under Castro as well). Together with U.S. Puerto Ricans, Cubans have the highest divorce rate of all Hispanic groups, and it is as high as within the non-Hispanic population.

POLITICAL ISSUES

Cubans in exile, the return to Cuba, and the fall of Castro.

Increased representation in U.S. politics.

HEALTH

Cubans may use household remedies and herbs that were used in Cuba.

They seek medical advice with greater frequency than other Hispanic groups.

Cuban adults rely less on vitamin-mineral supplements than any other Hispanic group and whites, and as little as blacks (U.S. Bureau of the Census, 1992a).

RELIGION

As with other Caribbean Hispanics, U.S. Cubans tend to be Catholic.

Cults are prevalent among Afro-Cubans. *Santeria* incorporates elements of Catholicism and Yoruba African cults. Belief is that *santeria* controls the forces of nature.

Santeros and *babalaos* (terms used in Miami, Tampa, and New York City) are equivalent to the *curanderos* in Mexico. They are spiritual healers or witches of African cults that were brought to the Caribbean during the 19th century.

Other differences among Christian U.S. Hispanic groups include variations in the image of Christ (Kanellos, 1993).

MUSIC

U.S. Cubans, like Puerto Ricans, Dominicans, and Afro-Cubans, share musical forms having Spanish and African roots. The salsa is the major component of Caribbean music.

The *danzon, rumba-guaguanco, charanga, mambo, guaracha, son, bolero,* and *cha-cha* all originated in Cuba.

U.S. Cubans

Salsa combines the styles of *son, rumba,* and *guaguanco* music. The style is distinctive for its call-and-response patterns between the soloist and the chorus. *Salsa* underwent more development in the United States with the infusion of jazz elements. *Salsa* has a strong cultural appeal to Caribbean Hispanics in the United States, as it is associated with religious performances in their homeland.

Latin jazz and Latin rock lack the Cuban cultural roots of salsa. It is said to be a creation of the commercial market. It has a great appeal to second-generation bilinguals (U.S.-born Hispanics).

LITERATURE

Has a long tradition in the United States but is more recent and less profuse than Mexican-American literature.

Written mostly in Spanish. Most recent prose characterized by its nostalgic and political content.

THEATER

U.S.-Cuban theater is more eclectic than Mexican theater. It incorporates several styles and genres, such as vaudeville, Broadway musical, bedroom farce, drama, Spanish versions of classics, and themes of anticommunism and Castro. Second-generation Cuban-American playwrights in New York seem to be less traditional than Miami playwrights.

SPORTS

Baseball. Large contribution of Cuban ball players to U.S. leagues.

FOODS

African and Spanish influences; tropical cuisine.

SECTION 4

CASE
HISTORIES

CASE STUDY

American Honda

CAMPAIGN   Capturing and Retaining the Leadership Position

BACKGROUND

In 1989 American Honda made a commitment to develop a program to market automobiles to the U.S. Hispanic market. The first step was to conduct a nationwide search for a Hispanic agency. Later that year, Honda picked La Agencia de Orci & Asociados in Los Angeles.

Honda's first challenge to La Agencia was to "earn the right to sell to Hispanics." Consequently, we spent the first several months in research and developing programs that would introduce Honda to the Hispanic market in a meaningful and long-term way.

RESEARCH

The 1989 Hispanic Honda owner was not a typical Hispanic. Before having a Hispanic program in place, Honda had been missing the bulk of the Hispanic new-car buyers, as evidenced in the profiles below.

1989 Honda Hispanic Owner	1989 Hispanic New-Car Buyer
Born in the U.S.	Born outside U.S.
Bilingual	Spanish dominant
Avg. HH Income $43,000	Avg. HH Income $32,000
Single	Married
<2 Children	2+ Children
Professional	Non-Professionals
College, some Post-Grad	High School, some College

Honda's Hispanic research also identified problems and opportunities.

THE PROBLEMS

There was low awareness of Honda. Though slowly gaining acceptance, imports were still perceived as undesirable. Hispanic consumers thought of them as:

> *Not elegant*
>
> *Small*
>
> *Underpowered*
>
> *Expensive to repair*
>
> *Basically inappropriate for the Hispanic family*

THE OPPORTUNITY

Hispanics who actually owned Hondas loved them, and saw them as:

> *Roomy*
>
> *Powerful*
>
> *Elegant*
>
> *Ideal for Hispanic families*

Research further confirmed that Hispanics wanted to be invited to buy, and to see themselves reflected in the advertising. Additionally, Hispanics wanted to see ads for the models they hoped to own: the top-of-the-line models, with all the features, the luxury and elegance they aspired to.

OBJECTIVES

To implement a dedicated program designed to:

> *Earn the right to sell to Hispanics*
>
> *Build a long-term relationship with the consumer*
>
> *Increase sales to Hispanics*
>
> *Provide sales growth opportunities for local dealers*

STRATEGY

We designed a 4-point strategy to build a long-term relationship with Hispanic consumers, as detailed below:

Cultural Enrichment

Community Support

Sports & Entertainment

Product Advertising

Cultural Enrichment

To celebrate the cultural gems that Latin America has contributed to this country, Honda became the founding sponsor of the Ballet Folklorico de Mexico's U.S. Tour. Since 1989, the annual 20-city tour has been deepening Honda's relationship to the Hispanic community.

Support includes:

TV ads in the top Hispanic markets (See Ballet TV Spot)

Radio/TV promotions and giveaways

Signage at the venue

Program ad

Print ads

Community Support

To demonstrate its interest in and support of issues important to the Hispanic community.

It was feared the Hispanic community would not fully participate in the Census, resulting in a significant population undercount. Participation was essential to get a fair share of federal support in the form of schools, hospitals, recreational facilities and representation. With this in mind, MALDEF (Mexican American Legal Defense and Educational Fund) came to Honda for support. Honda then set out to explain the benefits to Latinos of their being counted in the 1990 Census. (See '90 Census TV Spot)

As a result, Honda was recognized as a major contributor in generating the highest level of Hispanic participation in the 1990 Census, which led to increased representation of Hispanics in local and national government.

Sports and Entertainment Sponsorships

In order to win the hearts of Hispanic consumers, Honda began by supporting their favorite sports and entertainment. And by utilizing first-rate media vehicles, Honda strengthened its quality image.

Sports

Sponsoring major soccer events demonstrated Honda's knowledge of the consumer, and helped to deepen its rapport with the Hispanic community.

Also, innovative soccer crawls developed for Honda's sponsorship of the 1990 World Cup had great appeal for the target audience, and have changed the way the advertising industry now approaches crawl advertising.

World Cup Soccer Sponsor

Italia 1990 (See three 1990 crawls)

United States 1994 (See three 1994 crawls)

France 1998 (See three 1998 crawls)

Honda Player of the Year Award

> *Created in 1991, the Honda Award has become the most coveted award in U.S. professional soccer.*

Major League Soccer

> *1996–1999 exclusive automotive sponsor*

Sponsor of San Jose Clash team

Entertainment

From 1990 to 1999, Honda reached 1.1 million Hispanic homes each week through *Sabado Gigante*, the longest-running and highest-rated weekly show on Spanish-language television.

National sponsorship of "Sabado Gigante" since 1990

TV advertising

Product integration

Weekly opportunity to win a new Honda

A visible forum to support Honda's community involvement activities (See *Sabado Gigante* footage)

Product Advertising

Product advertising began in 1990, a full year after initiating activities on the strategic points described above. The advertising was designed to appeal to specific Hispanic needs, and to establish a relevant and aspirational image for each Honda model.

Over the years, we have added models to the Hispanic line-up, and have refined product positionings for each model to enhance their appeal to specific target segments. In 1999, they are as follows:

- **Civic Coupe**

   Target: Up & coming young Hispanics

   Positioning: "The perfect car for all your adventures."

   (See *Civic Coupe '99* "Mission")

- **Civic Sedan**

   Target: Young Hispanic families

   Positioning: "Excitement and styling in a family sedan."

   (See *Civic Sedan '99* "It's Your Style")

- **Accord Sedan**

   Target: Mature, more affluent adults

   Positioning: "Rewards your success and accomplishments."

   (See *Accord Sedan '99* "Through a Child's Eyes")

• **Odyssey Mini-Van**

Target: Established Hispanic families with 2+ kids

Positioning: "A pleasurable family experience."

(See *Odyssey '99* "A Valet's Dream")

RESULTS

The results of our Hispanic program are enviable. Not only is Honda the number-one-selling passenger car brand, the Civic and the Accord are the top-two-selling car models in the Hispanic market, according to R.L. Polk. In fact, in 1990, the Accord reached the number one position in sales to Hispanics after only one year of product advertising.

Honda has had the #1 and #2 selling models 8 years in a row!

	'89	'90	'91	'92	'93	'94	'95	'96	'97	'98
Accord	#5	#1	#1	#1	#2	#2	#2	#2	#2	#1
Civic	#4	#3	#2	#2	#1	#1	#1	#1	#1	#2

Further, our research tells us that in addition to being a sales success, we have built and nurtured a solid brand with a loyal consumer franchise. (See current image Focus Group footage)

CASE STUDY

JCPenney

JCPenney®

CAMPAIGN

Floralace® Lingerie

BACKGROUND

Recently, the landscape of the retail apparel market has undergone significant change. The marketplace has become more complex with the diversification of the retail environment. Mass merchandisers and discounters as well as specialty stores have become strong competition for traditional department stores. JCPenney understands that newcomers like Victoria's Secret® and other specialty lingerie stores, as well as Target and Wal-Mart, are aggressively seeking increased market share. Consumers are drawn to those retailers who specifically target them and provide the fashions for their specific lifestyle or mindset. JCPenney offers these relevant fashions. JCPenney is one of the top retailers of intimate apparel in America in the department store category, and it is imperative that retailers like JCPenney react to this competitive marketplace.

CAMPAIGN OBJECTIVES

Marketing Objective

To increase the sales of lingerie during the JCPenney Lingerie Sale period.

Communications Objectives

> To introduce the new Floralace brand of lingerie and establish the collection as a viable fashion brand available to suit specific needs of the JCPenney target.
>
> To enhance the image of JCPenney as a lingerie shopping destination for Hispanics.

Target Audience

> Hispanic, African-American, and Anglo females, aged 18 to 49

STRATEGY

In May 1999 JCPenney asked its Hispanic advertising agency, Cartel Creativo Inc., to work closely with the African-American agency to create a lingerie brand commercial that was only to air on two award shows—the Hispanic Alma Awards on ABC and the African-American Essence Awards also airing on ABC. The Lingerie brand TV spot was created to continue to build the image of JCPenney's Lingerie department as well as communicate to the target audience the great new Floralace Lingerie Collection by Delicates® available at JCPenney.

INSIGHT

Cartel Creativo recognized that there were some definite cultural similarities among women of different non-Anglo ethnic backgrounds. The "New Marianismo" theory (*The Maria Paradox,* Gil and Vazquez, Putnam's, 1996) states that many U.S. Hispanic females (like African-American women) are finding a balance between their beloved traditional social values and their emerging independence and self-expression. Fashion, including lingerie, is simply another extension of this self-expression.

CREATIVE EXECUTION

Cartel then produced an English-language ethnically targeted lingerie brand TV spot that included Hispanic as well as African-American talent. Instead of the typical lingerie advertising that seems to be addressed more to the male than the female, the agency opted to create a connection with the female who is looking for comfort and style, as well as lingerie that gives them personal pleasure. The spot ends with the words. . . "And men think we buy lingerie just for them!"

EVIDENCE OF RESULTS

The commercial was favorably received by the client and the decision was then made to take this brand spot, which was originally created for the ethnic target, and run it concurrently (with a sales message adaptation) with another sales-oriented lingerie TV commercial during a Lingerie sale event in May 1999. The spot contributed to a 26 percent increase in total lingerie sales for JCPenney.

CASE STUDY

La Opinión

CAMPAIGN

La Opinión Expands Market Reach Through Joint Distribution Partnership with the *Los Angeles Times*

La Opinión, the country's leading Spanish-language daily newspaper, made a giant leap forward in penetrating the growing Southern California Latino market through a joint distribution and marketing program with the *Los Angeles Times.*

Starting on August 2nd, in a cross-over promotion like one never before seen in Los Angeles, *La Opinión* and the *Los Angeles Times* partnered to distribute both papers together, an undeniable recognition of the changing demographics in Southern California that sets a precedent for continued efforts to satisfy the needs and wants of the Latino families across the United States.

For a period of nine weeks, the *Los Angeles Times* was inserted into nearly all copies of *La Opinión,* and distributed throughout the Southern California region, including non-core areas for *La Opinión,* like Riverside, Ventura and San Diego counties.

Marketed under the slogan banner *Para Todos y Cada Uno* (For Each and Everyone), the bundled papers are sold for 35 cents at *La Opinión* news racks and retailers; *La Opinión* is also available as a stand-alone product in certain areas for 25 cents.

The new product serves the needs of both readers and advertisers. For advertisers, it provides the unique vehicle they have been looking for to effectively reach the growing number of bilingual Latino households.

For consumers, the venture gives readers the best of both worlds. As the local Hispanic marketplace becomes increasingly bilingual, it offers readers the opportunity to enjoy two great newspapers in one convenient package.

The joint promotion was launched with an aggressive advertising campaign on August 16 to promote the paper's joint distribution with the *Los Angeles Times*. The campaign included TV, radio, newspaper, point-of-purchase, bus shelters and Internet advertising.

The advertising campaign captured perfectly the purpose for the promotion: to reach the growing number of bilingual households, using emotional and innovative communication elements that are common to both cultures.

STRATEGY

The creative, developed by cruz/kravetz:IDEAS, *La Opinión*'s agency of record, included a 30-second TV spot executed in an animated comic format using human-like characters that reflect the social and ethnic diversity of the Hispanic bilingual market. The execution used an animation technique that treats movement of different layers within the same frame independently, combined with optical perspective tricks and sophisticated sound effects. The 60-second radio spot, complementing the TV film, emulates a movie trailer. The tone of the spots was inspired by thriller movie sound effects and adventure comic aesthetics.

MEDIA

The TV and radio spots were aired on all Hispanic TV stations and the majority of Hispanic radio stations during a 6-week flight. In-paper ads ran in *La Opinión* and the *Los Angeles Times* for 9 weeks, and full-size posters were displayed at 145 bus shelters in selected locations.

Through this promotion, readers receive *La Opinión*'s outstanding coverage in sports, entertainment and Hispanic news, now complemented with the *Los Angeles Times* coverage of general information. This program was designed as the most practical and convenient approach to serving the changing demographics of the Southern California marketplace. Most importantly, it introduced *La Opinión* to new readers throughout the Southern California market.

According to industry sources, Southern California ranks as the country's largest Hispanic market with a population in excess of 6.5 million and $67 billion in purchasing power. Advertisers spent more than $68 million reaching the market just in Los Angeles County in 1997.

At the same time, the market is becoming increasingly bilingual. Recent studies indicate that 35 percent of Hispanic readers prefer bilingual content, while 36 percent of households are fully bilingual and 31 percent speak Spanish only.

RESULTS

La Opinión is the nation's largest Spanish-language daily newspaper, with a daily circulation of 107,000. *La Opinión* was founded on September 16, 1926, and is based in Los Angeles. It circulates throughout the five-county Southern California area and reaches over half a million readers. The paper has been published by the Lozano family since its founding. The paper has also established marketing partnerships with KMEX-TV, Grupo Gigante supermarkets and Radio Unica to fully penetrate the Hispanic market.

CASE STUDY

El Pollo Loco

1999 CAMPAIGN TITLE

Romancing the Chicken

MARKETING CONTEXT

Until the third quarter of 1998, El Pollo Loco's positioning was fragmented, and it considered its competitors to include: Taco Bell, Del Taco, McDonald's, Burger King, Pizza Hut and Subway, as well as KFC, Boston Market, and Popeye's—in short, every type of restaurant in the fast-food category. Consequently, its advertising, promotion and pricing reflected this fragmented approach. One spot would emphasize variety, another value and, yet another, child appeal. Additionally, ten promotions were scheduled throughout the year with insufficient media dollars to adequately support either their delivery or their objective to generate immediate awareness of any one of them. As a result, sales declined significantly during several quarters prior to the featured campaign period, while other fast-food chains continued to see gains. Specifically, Hispanic sales volume had decreased for two consecutive years; -0.8 percent between 1996 and 1997 and -2.0 percent between 1997 and 1998.

The challenges to cruz/kravetz:IDEAS were several. The first was to get the client refocused on its core product: Marinated and flame-broiled chicken. It seemed that, in its quest to be "all things to all people," it had forgotten its "reason for being" in the first place. The second challenge was to develop advertising which would help deliver this new positioning, while also delivering the promotional call to action so important to building traffic during promotional periods. Focus group research indicated that El Pollo Loco had successfully held onto strong consumer perceptions of Flavor/Taste and Food Quality and Value, so we knew we were on the right track. Third, the campaign had to capitalize on the "Fresh Mex" craze by emphasizing El Pollo Loco's inherently fresh and healthy approach to Mexican food. Thus, the agency worked to re-define and narrow El Pollo Loco's positioning and, in turn, its competitive set. Since this new positioning work was undertaken and adopted by El Pollo Loco, the direction has also been adopted by the client's general-market (non-Hispanic) agency.

CAMPAIGN PLANNING

Focus groups were conducted as were intercept interviews at various El Pollo Loco locations in high Hispanic density neighborhoods. In addition, observational research was conducted, not only of how consumers interacted with the El Pollo Loco environment and its employees, but also its menu boards, point-of-sale, eating and parking facilities, and drive-though service. Further, in-depth analysis was prepared of Quick Track, the category quarterly syndicated study. This study allowed us to determine where El Pollo Loco stood relative to its "true" competition in terms of awareness, ad awareness, usage and product attributes. It also helped to confirm that our planned creative approach would be believable.

Target Market

California

Target Audience

El Pollo Loco's target audience for this campaign consisted of Hispanic adults aged 18 to 49. They are fast-food users and tend to frequent fast-food chains 8 to 12 times per month. In terms of language, they are Spanish-dominant and/or Spanish-preferred. The majority are married, and eight in ten have children in the household. These families are very traditional and, for the most part, tend to eat at home. This is due to Hispanic families' affinity for home-cooked traditional meals. These are people who maintain the culture of the "old" country, yet are also acculturating to America. And, because they are dual-earner households, the concept of affordable home meal replacement is becoming more and more attractive to them. El Pollo Loco is a perfect fit for this consumer because it offers chicken marinated and flame-broiled in a traditional Mexican manner. The chain of more than 200 restaurants was, in fact, founded by a Mexican immigrant in 1980 and was acquired by Denny's Inc. in 1983. Both El Pollo Loco and Denny's were ultimately sold to Advantica several years later.

CAMPAIGN OBJECTIVES

The objective was to re-capture those consumers who had left El Pollo Loco, not necessarily because they stopped liking the product, but because El Pollo Loco had not given them a motivating reason to stop by, vis-à-vis the competition. Bottom line: the campaign had to make the target crave the chicken again, reverse the sales declines and place El Pollo Loco back on a growth track. More specifically, El Pollo Loco had to show increased Hispanic volume results.

Marketing Strategy

El Pollo Loco's new marketing strategy was to focus on the chicken—its core product and strength—and to remind people of its great taste. The campaign had to stimulate trial and repeat usage. We knew from focus groups that when we talked about the El Pollo Loco experience, it triggered all sorts of sensory reactions. Consumers could imagine the taste, the smell, and even the sound of the chicken on the grill. They could even imagine the steam rising from the freshly flame-broiled chicken.

Communication Strategy

Knowing how consumers reacted to the chicken, even when only talking about it, compelled us to find a way to impart the necessary stimuli through the campaign in order to create the same reaction when watching or hearing the commercials at home. This strategy was meant to be very sensory-driven and one that would speak to and pull on consumers' "stomach strings." The new positioning read, "El Pollo Loco stimulates my senses because only they marinate and flame-broil their chicken to mouth-watering perfection."

Media Strategy

Media were strategically planned and purchased to generate immediate awareness and support five key promotions for the 1999 marketing calendar. Media were planned and bought to coincide with time periods leading into lunch and dinner meal times. A combination of television :30s and :15s were utilized to increase media weight levels and maximize the number of on-air weeks. Radio was used to drive the campaign's frequency especially during afternoon drive time. Additionally, the focus was placed on programming that delivered high reach versus frequency, and careful spot placement was considered when placing media schedules. Leveraged merchandising was a key element to this campaign in which we negotiated billboard sponsorships, upgrades, bonus spots, off-site event participation, on-air promotions and product integration. Media flight weeks were planned to start at the beginning of each module and then stair-stepped to help maximize the number of on-air weeks to provide continuity and to support all key modules.

Creative Approach

The creative approach was to "romance" the chicken visually on camera and verbally on radio. The idea was to leverage the possible imagery through sight and sound. The chicken was romanced by playing on double meanings in well-known, romantic Spanish-language ballads. We made them sing to the chicken about "not being able to live without you," about "being unforgettable" and about "being the only important one."

EVIDENCE OF RESULTS

The repositioning and resulting creative strategy and approach resulted in very strong Hispanic sales volume increases. Overall, during a 36-week period vs. year-ago, El Pollo Loco has seen a Hispanic volume increase of 7.2 percent. This is 250 percent above El Pollo Loco's 2 percent target increase year-to-date. Further, weekly Hispanic sales volume increases have been as high as 10.1 percent for El Pollo Loco, as was the case during the eight-week Barbecue Chicken promotion—not typically a traditional flavoring for chicken among Hispanics. The campaign was measured through El Pollo Loco's proprietary sales tracking system.

CASE STUDY

House Foods Corporation

CAMPAIGN

How House Foods Sold Japanese Curry to Hispanics

July–September 1999

BACKGROUND

House Foods America is a subsidiary of House Foods Corporation, a Japanese packaged-foods company that sells a variety of products in the U.S., including seasonings, gelatins, tofu and Japanese-style curry. Except for tofu, most of their products are sold primarily in small, Asian specialty stores. In an effort to grow volume, House Foods approached cruz/kravetz:IDEAS to look into the feasibility of launching Java Curry, a Japanese-style curry, into the Hispanic market in Los Angeles.

PLANNING RESEARCH

Focus groups and follow-up phone interviews for in-home product placement and trial indicated that Hispanics loved the taste of the product. The spicy flavor was especially appealing and compared favorably with Mexican style Mole. Further, it was found that Java Curry's "bouillon cube" formulation aligned with the already high incidence of food flavoring and spice usage. In fact, Java Curry is identical to bouillon cubes in consistency so the product felt familiar to participants.

However, reactions to the product packaging were negative. Research indicated that Hispanics found the existing packaging and product shot unappealing and Java Curry, the existing name, was meaningless to them. In addition, respondents also said that the packaging did not provide much information about the product.

THE CHALLENGE

The product was re-packaged and introduced to the Hispanic market as "House Curry Casero."

The initial challenge for cruz/kravetz:IDEAS was to recommend a new name and provide an assessment and recommendations for a package re-design. Focus groups were again conducted to test various names and packaging designs. As a result the product was introduced to the Hispanic market as "House Curry Casero" and the new packaging was considered more appealing because among other things, the food looked better, it included more product information and graphically explained its preparation.

However, the biggest challenges were yet to come. First, the product was new and manufactured by an unfamiliar company. Until then, the product had only been sold through Asian specialty stores. Consequently, neither retailers nor consumers were familiar with it. Second, consumers would be limited in their ability to include it in their cooking routines. Third, the budget was limited; therefore, TV was not an option. Both media and creative were challenged to develop an effective campaign that would maximize a budget under $250,000.

TARGET AUDIENCE

Hispanic females aged 18 to 49, with children

Primary shopper in the household

Spanish-dominant

Cook from scratch

Heavy users of seasonings, spices and bouillon cube/powder-based product.

Hispanics were selected as the target due to their importance in the Los Angeles market. Evidence of their importance is reflected in the overall media ratings where Spanish-language radio and TV stations have consistently been in the top ratings for the last few years. In addition, more than 38.7 percent of the total population in the Los Angeles DMA is Hispanic, totaling 6.3 million. In fact, approximately 21 percent of all Hispanics in the U.S. live in the Los Angeles DMA. The target was narrowed to Hispanic females because it was deemed important to reach the person who was most influential in making purchases and preparing meals for the Hispanic family.

MARKETING STRATEGY

An advertising and promotions program was developed with a two-fold purpose. First, the program was meant to generate awareness and trial for the product, and second, but more importantly, it was designed to leverage shelf space through in-store demos, point-of-sale, free-standing-inserts, coupon handouts, and retailer-specific tags and radio remotes. Recipe brochures were developed and designed to put the product into the context of Hispanic cooking styles and to familiarize and make the consumer comfortable with the product. The media buy was leveraged to extend the product's exposure through on-air taste testing and through taste testing with food editors at newspapers like *La Opinión*, which ended up writing an editorial piece on the product and the recipes.

DISTRIBUTION STRATEGY

Hispanics in the LA area tend to shop in small, independent stores as well as chain retailers, but we knew that without a lot of money, it would be almost impossible to get distribution in the chains from the beginning, so we targeted independent retailers with at least 50 percent Hispanic customer base first. This was a crucial factor in the strategy because it would allow us to prove that the product would sell so we could then leverage the success to obtain distribution in the large retail chains.

MEASUREMENT

Because in-store research measurement vehicles that track store sales for larger chains do not cover many independent grocery stores, it was determined that results were to be measured primarily through distribution—gains in the total number of stores selling the product. Secondary measures of success would include total sampling activity, sales feedback and coupon redemption. In fact, sampling and couponing would also be used strategically to secure product distribution and would be aligned with media flight dates.

PROGRAM ELEMENTS

Media

In an ideal situation, television would have been considered the best vehicle to introduce this product because it serves as a visual medium to introduce an unfamiliar product. With a budget of under $250,000, TV was not a viable option. The media campaign lasted five weeks and supported the initial launch. It consisted of radio and run-of-press advertising (ROPs) which dropped in local Spanish newspapers.

Added value was negotiated with radio stations and included on-air tastings, remotes, advertorials featuring House Curry Casero recipes and 10-second banners which sponsored radio segments such as Chef Parra, who provided daily recipes on-air.

In-store Sampling

In-store activity was crucial to the product's success for several reasons. First, it served as leverage to gain in-store access. This is especially important for a brand like

House Curry Casero which is manufactured by a company that is not well known in the U.S., though it has numerous strong brands in Japan. In-store demos served to encourage stores to stock the product.

Second, it allowed customers to sample the product and ask questions about the product. Incentives such as savings coupons and gifts with purchase were also used to drive sales. Point-of-sale material in the form of posters and danglers was designed to support the in-store activity. Recipes using House Curry Casero were customized to meet the preferences and cooking styles of the Hispanic market.

COMMUNICATION STRATEGY

The biggest barrier House Curry Casero needed to overcome was that consumers were not familiar with the product nor did they know how to use/prepare it. Communications strategy needed to focus on communicating taste appeal of the product and its uses. The strategy needed to let customers know that:

House Curry Casero tastes great

The family would love it

A key insight was that Hispanics generally do not want to sacrifice homemade taste when using an easy-to-make product. Hispanic women cook more often than other segments and take great pride in preparing homemade meals and taking care of and pleasing their families. The fact that the product was easy to make would therefore be a secondary incentive and not the primary purchase motivator. The communication needed to convince Hispanic consumers to try something new and convince them that House Curry Casero was a familiar flavor with an exotic touch.

CREATIVE

It was important for the advertising to convey taste appeal and inform consumers about House Curry Casero and product preparation and serving instructions.

The key ideas communicated were as follows:

> *The product has a great homemade taste and contains a delicious blend of spices*
>
> *Your whole family will love it*
>
> *It's easy to prepare with meat, chicken or fish and your favorite vegetables*
>
> *It comes in two varieties: Mild (Sazonado) and Hot (Picosito)*

EVIDENCE OF RESULTS

Distribution in 50 independent stores in July and August.

Distribution in 80 Food 4 Less stores as of September 1999.

Vons and Ralphs have now agreed to carry the product, beginning November 1999.

1,944 packages were sold through in-store sampling activity from July 1999 to September 1999.

Client has increased marketing budget to include TV by the end of the year.

CASE STUDY

California Lincoln Mercury Dealers Association (CLMDA)

1999 CAMPAIGN TITLE

The People Who Move California

MARKETING CONTEXT

January 1999 was the first time that CLMDA had developed any type of Spanish-language marketing campaign targeting Hispanics. Overall, car sales to Hispanics in California had increased by 9.2 percent from 1997 to 1998 (Mercury segments only, CYTD July), while Mercury had seen a decrease in Hispanic sales of 13.8 percent. The challenge to cruz/kravetz:IDEAS was to develop a campaign that provided the "hard sell" necessary to drive traffic into dealer showrooms during key sales periods, but also to promote the image and help generate awareness of Mercury vehicles. Dealer association advertising normally does not have this dual role. However, because of the national Hispanic campaign's ineffectiveness and irrelevance and the lack of Mercury awareness among the target consumer, it became evident that fulfilling this dual role would be necessary. Further, we were challenged by the following "realities":

• Dealerships are not staffed to service Hispanic consumers; almost no bilingual sales people and no written materials in Spanish.

• Many dealerships are dual dealerships (i.e., Ford/ Lincoln Mercury, Volvo/Lincoln Mercury, etc.). This left the decision of which car to push in the hands of a salesperson.

- In many cases, especially with Ford, Hispanics are persuaded away from Mercury vehicles and towards the comparable and less expensive Ford to close a sale.

- Among those who are familiar with Mercury, it was seen as being a slightly "better" brand than Ford, but consumers did not know why. They also felt that the Ford was the same as the Mercury, but that it offered more value for the price.

CAMPAIGN PLANNING

Because budget parameters did not allow for primary research, the agency conducted an extensive analysis of all existing qualitative and quantitative research and use account planning disciplines such as one-on-one interviews with consumers and dealer personnel. The research indicated that Hispanic consumers' awareness of the Mercury brand and its vehicles was non-existent. Further, the "Imagine yourself in a Mercury" campaign currently in place for national general and Hispanic markets was not being understood by and was irrelevant among Hispanics at this stage in the brand's life cycle. More important, it did not deliver on the core values the target considered important and on which, we knew, Mercury models could deliver. Our conclusion was that the advertising's original, client-intended direction of adapting to and adopting elements of the national image campaign would have to change to make this campaign successful. We presented our case and the client ultimately approved the recommended direction to move away from the national umbrella campaign.

Target Markets

California

Target Audience

The primary target was affluent Hispanic adults with household incomes of over $50,000, who are most likely to purchase Mercury vehicles today. The secondary target was upwardly mobile Hispanic households for future brand and model consideration. This target was the focus because Lincoln Mercury is a luxury brand that appeals to an upscale consumer. The idea was to align the brand with the "inspirational" in order to target the affluent consumer, yet appeal to the growing population of middle-class Hispanics through their aspirational tendencies.

CAMPAIGN OBJECTIVES

Although the original charge was "dealer advertising," it was decided that the advertising had to be just as effective at creating a positioning for each of the models, as it would be at increasing brand and model consideration, in order to achieve an increase in qualified dealer traffic. The campaign's effectiveness was measured by R.L. Polk Hispanic Registrations. We believed that sales were the only true measure of a successful dealer campaign.

MARKETING AND COMMUNICATION STRATEGIES

The marketing strategy was driven through a focus on the Cougar, Mountaineer, and Villager; the three most likely models to appeal to Hispanics. These are also the Mercury flagship models. The idea was to derive inspiration from, and aspiration to, Mercury vehicles. Further, at a grass roots level, the brand and the models were aligned with Hispanic targeted events and activities which were upscale and trendy, and where the vehicles could be displayed. Entertainment was a focus for these activities (i.e., comedy shows, concerts) to align the Mercury brand with a lifestyle that is fun and upscale. The communication strategy centered on conveying the brand essence for each model and for the Mercury brand as a whole. These essences were created to parallel the target's core values as they relate to each of the featured car segments. The following essences were developed for the Mercury brand and for each of the target vehicles:

Mercury Brand

Mercury embodies and delivers what California's diverse consumers want from a car because only Mercury captures and understands their human essence and spirit.

Cougar

The Mercury Cougar is uncompromising, it exudes power and it is decisive. When I drive the Cougar, I can push life to the edge and cut through any obstacles because I can feel its guts, its soul and its passion for control.

Mountaineer

The Mercury Mountaineer is bold, adventurous and fearless. When I drive the Mountaineer, I can conquer the world, wild or tame, because it gives me the freedom and confidence to go anywhere, anytime.

Villager

The Mercury Villager is real, it's honest and unpretentious. When I drive the Mercury Villager, I can handle life's realities because I feel protected by its soothing and safe embrace. With it, I can overcome the everyday challenges, big and small, directly and with confidence.

MEDIA STRATEGY

Media was strategically planned and bought to place the campaign during prime viewing hours, targeting programs that skewed to and which would generate the greatest awareness among the affluent Hispanic target. Television and radio drove campaign delivery in Northern and Southern California. Spots were placed in news and entertainment programming on television. International, romantic, and ballad music formats were chosen on radio. Merchandising was negotiated in the form of bonus spots, sponsorship billboards, and remotes. All added value aired in and around the same type of programming. Media flights were concentrated during promotional and key holiday periods throughout the year. This allowed Mercury to promote specific sales incentives and generate the greatest amount of awareness during time periods when Hispanic consumers would be most likely to purchase.

CREATIVE APPROACH

The television executions were developed using "running footage" due to budget constraints. The notion was to take the footage and, through editing, graphics, supers, sound effects, and music, impart a specific personality to each model. Original music was developed to obtain an emotional response to the personality of each of the focus vehicles as well as impart an upbeat Latino feel. Overall, the approach was to create an image that Mercury cars were alive and ready to take the target wherever they wanted to go, physically and emotionally.

RESULTS

Overall, during the six-month period in which the campaign aired and from which results from R.L. Polk are available, California Hispanic sales for the Mercury brand increased by 31.9 percent versus 1.0 percent decrease for same period, year-ago (YAG). Comparatively, non-Hispanic sales increased by only 10.8 percent during the same period. Cougar, Mercury's new model, drove the sales increase. Mountaineer also saw a 12 percent increase in Hispanic sales versus a 10 percent decrease in non-Hispanic sales. The Villager saw a slight decrease of 3 percent in Hispanic sales while non-Hispanic sales suffered more dramatically with a 13 percent decline. These three models were the core vehicles featured in the advertising during the first half of 1999. During this same time period in 1998, Hispanic sales made up 8.6 percent of total California Lincoln Mercury sales. In 1999, Hispanic sales grew to represent 11 percent of total California Lincoln Mercury sales.

In measuring the success of this campaign, it is also important to note the performance of the Lincoln vehicles during this same time period. While sales of Mercury vehicles were clearly the ultimate goal of this campaign, the initial objective was to drive qualified traffic into dealer showroom. Because all Mercury dealerships in California are also Lincoln dealerships, driving traffic into the dealership through Mercury advertising also generated sales of the Lincoln vehicles. Sales of Lincoln vehicles to Hispanics during this time frame increased by 17.9 percent, compared with a decrease of 21.2 percent among non-Hispanics. This success among Hispanics in the Sports Specialty and SUV segments have led Lincoln Mercury to include the new LS and the Navigator in the core vehicle set for model year 2000. This will be Lincoln's first-ever effort to target Hispanic consumers.

CASE STUDY

Paragon Cable San Antonio

FOREWORD

Until the mid-to-late 1990s (with the growth of "direct-to-home" satellite services), one might have assumed that cable television systems had no direct competition. In a broad sense, however, they do compete for dollars with many other forms of entertainment. One of the interesting aspects of this case was this realization and the incorporation of this competitive element in the creative strategy and executions, especially as it relates to the attribute of "value."

Most cable systems had reached the point of market penetration (70 percent and higher) where signing up new subscribers became difficult and costly. Since Hispanic cable penetrations generally ran anywhere from 10 percent to 25 percent below non-Hispanic subscription levels, many systems had come to recognize this market as an area of considerable opportunity. In fact, in some franchise areas, in order to grow, the majority of the new subscriptions had to come from Hispanic residents and/or other low-penetration market segments.

Another interesting aspect of this campaign was that spots were created in both languages, airing on local Spanish and English-language TV stations in the market. The San Antonio DMA is over 50 percent Hispanic. The goal of this marketing effort was to cover the entire market, reaching non-Hispanics as well as Hispanics—be it in Spanish or in English.

Although this meant that not all of the new subscribers could be categorized as "Hispanics," based on the cable system's analysis of neighborhoods where the new "sign-ups" came from—of surnames and of the number of phone calls handled in Spanish—the majority of these new subscribers were, indeed, Hispanics.

MARKETING BACKGROUND

While the cable industry has flourished, Hispanic subscription rates have not kept pace. One reason for the disparity has been the issue of perceived value of cable service. A common Hispanic reaction is, "Why should I get cable if I can watch free TV?" Two Hispanic consumer misperceptions identified by Cartel Creativo were that . . .

. . . There were few added offerings (or, at least, few worthwhile offerings) over and above what one could currently watch on "over-the-air" channels. Having never subscribed to cable, many Hispanics had limited knowledge of what programming services the local system carried.

. . . It was perceived as a luxury. A cable subscription was expensive. As mentioned, many had no first-hand cable subscription experience. It was not unusual for these Hispanics to estimate a subscription in the $30 or higher range.

In spite of these misconceptions, one enduring fact stood out—Hispanics love television. As documented by Nielsen ratings, Hispanic households spend significantly more time than average households using television each day. And, with larger households (and as supported by a number of other research sources), they spend disproportionate dollars on entertainment. In addition, Hispanics are attuned to learning about new, family-oriented entertainment vehicles. One of the enduring objectives had to be to change their negative perceptions in a nice, friendly way.

Based on this information, Cartel Creativo created an acquisition campaign for Paragon Cable San Antonio. It was decided to kick off this campaign in the month of July, a historically slow cable acquisition period.

TRACKING AND MEASUREMENT

Paragon Cable has the ability to accurately measure the results of their advertising campaigns by using "campaign codes" for each new campaign. As consumers call in, give the appropriate code and order cable service, Paragon is quickly able to assess effectiveness of each new advertising/marketing effort.

A new cable client is not "tallied" until after service has been installed in the customer's place of residence.

PARAGON CABLE AD BRIEF: OVERVIEW

According to Simmons Marketing Research Bureau (SMRB), national cable penetration stood at around 70 percent for the general market and at 47 percent for Hispanics. In San Antonio, low-penetration areas were identified in the south, east and west sides of the market. Paragon saw tremendous market potential in these largely Hispanic areas.

Non-subscribers fall into two general categories: former subscribers (including many who sign up and cancel periodically) and non-subscribers who have never had cable. This latter segment dominated in the identified neighborhoods/areas. It was also the segment specifically targeted for this advertising effort. For Paragon Cable, in terms of expanding their customer base, this segment represented a significant opportunity for growth.

First-time subscription is a big step for the consumer. Pushing someone to take that step required a compelling, informative and logical approach. There was "inertia" to overcome, and in a sense, a form of complacency. On the other hand, the experience of the system and the agency suggested that, although these prospects may kick, scream, scratch, and bite before subscribing, once "converted"—once exposed to the variety of programming services and the inherent value—they would just as passionately maintain that subscription.

COMMUNICATION STRATEGY

The principal misconception advertising had to overcome was lack of perceived value.

The benefits advertising had to communicate:

When competitive factors were weighed, other forms of entertainment were more expensive. Cable was affordable, personal, innovative, even inspiring. It could expand your world.

The goal was to communicate that:

> *Cable was not an unattainable luxury*
>
> *As a form of entertainment, it represented an excellent value*
>
> *Paragon Cable was the best source of entertainment in town*

The aim was to drive the consumer to consider Paragon Cable, to come to the realization that the combination of programming offerings and low price (value) represented something very special—something they had been missing out on. The existing mindset, "I can watch my favorite programs just fine with my antenna; and besides, cable is too expensive," needed to be attacked. The issue of inertia/complacency was key. The communication needed to be compelling enough to get them to act.

CAMPAIGN OBJECTIVES

A specific objective was defined at the outset. This objective: To increase the number of Paragon Cable subscribers by 3,500 homes in July 1997 and 3,500 more homes in August. A secondary goal was to retain new customers "forever"—to make them "cable addicts."

Target Audience

Adults (with a female skew) in households with at least $24,000 annual income

Primary demographic: *25-to-34-year-olds*
Secondary demographic: *30-to-54-year-olds*

Media

The logical vehicle for reaching potential cable subscribers was local television. Spanish and English versions of the spots were created, airing on both Spanish and English-language stations in San Antonio. The spots ran during July and August, with "heavy" media weight. Direct mail supported the TV. Orders were handled by customer representatives who answered in both Spanish and English.

CREATIVE EXECUTION

The advertising needed to be bold, arresting-enough to affect behavioral change—to overcome complacency—while sticking to "the basics." To ensure memorability and the ability to cut through "clutter," spots could not be dull or boring. A light-hearted comedic approach was used to show the absurdity of not having cable. The message: "Get it!" (Get hip/get cable). In Spanish, *Conéctate!* (Get connected/get connected to cable).

Commercials built their foundation around three basic themes:

> *The great value of cable*
>
> *Better reception*
>
> *Great programming*
>
> The first spots (airing in July) especially emphasized the $12 introductory rate.

Key copy points were:

> *Basic Cable is available for only $12 a month*
>
> *Nobody should be without cable*
>
> *No more excuses*
>
> *Nobody should be watching a fuzzy picture*
>
> *You're missing out on a lot*
>
> *Without cable, you're the equivalent of a "nerd"*

RESULTS

New "connects" for July exceeded the 3,500 goal by 213 percent. They surpassed the previous July total by 57 percent. And, in spite of the focus on the low-cost basic service package, most of these new customers opted for upgrades—two-thirds included one or more premium services in their subscription (HBO, Showtime, Cinemax, Disney, etc.)

Interestingly, the campaign from the prior July featured a premium package offer (while this new one featured the basic package), yet the number and proportion signing up for premium service in this new campaign exceeded the year-ago numbers.

Results for the August campaign were similarly successful. The goal of 3,500 new subscribers was exceeded by 203 percent. It represented a 405 percent increased, compared with the prior August, and the number opting for premium service far exceeded the prior August total.

Paragon was extremely happy with these results. To quote Paragon's marketing director at the time:

> "This is one of our most successful acquisition campaigns ever. We have nearly achieved year-end goal and it's only September! Much of this growth is attributable to the strategic campaign Cartel Creativo created which ran in the months of July and August, two months that have been historically low in new connects."

CASE STUDY

Tecate®

CAMPAIGN

Tecate® 1998

BACKGROUND

Since it first became available in the U.S. in the early 1970s, Mexican import Tecate® beer had achieved steady momentum in terms of U.S. volume share. However, aggressive marketing efforts and large budgets from domestic brewing giants continued to impede Hispanic purchasing by attempting to break down their preferences and consumption of import beers.

At the time, the Tecate® creative campaign focused on "A Taste of Mexico." Targeting Mexican Americans, it attempted to position Tecate® as everything that is Mexican, evoking images and memories of traditional Mexican music, food and other important cultural icons.

To the recent immigrant from Mexico now living in the U.S., however, life was vastly different and more challenging than what "A Taste of Mexico" had to offer. Just like its core consumer, Tecate® was trying to find its niche in the beer industry. Consequently, Tecate® focused its efforts on increasing the market share within the Mexican-American market.

OBJECTIVE

In 1998, the objectives were to gain volume-share among Spanish-dominant, U.S. Mexican Americans, particularly those born in Mexico, and to continue to collect additional insight into the Mexican-American segment of the Hispanic market.

MARKETING CHALLENGE

The marketing communications challenge to Cartel Creativo, therefore, was to build brand loyalty by:

• Portraying the product in a winning light and establishing recognition for the brand

• Making a parallel to the core consumers' experiences and realities of life in the U.S.

• Increasing awareness and designing the advertising message to drive preference of Tecate during the key sales seasons

• Reaching the core consumer through a highly targeted and focused media effort

MEDIA STRATEGIES

With this in mind, Tecate® launched its 1998 *Llego, para quedarse* (Here, to Stay) campaign.

The campaign focused on Spanish-dominant, Mexican-American male consumers.

It was a highly cost-efficient approach that combined national network TV sponsorships, promotional/branding radio spots, and outdoor overlays with priority-market emphasis.

Media Tactics

The TV strategy centered on ensured visibility through property ownership (category exclusivity). All TV sponsorship properties were focused on sports and entertainment programming, with a combined reach that totaled over 60 percent of the target.

Network TV was selected to provide year-round presence for the brand. Cable TV sports programming was selected due to its strong inventory of Spanish-language soccer properties.

Increased awareness and brand exposure were the goals of outdoor executions. This impactful program featured 8-sheet, 30-sheet and 14' × 48' boards in areas with high densities of Mexican Americans.

Radio stations with exclusively Mexican regional music formats were selected (i.e., Ranchera, Norteña, Banda and Grupo).

PROMOTIONAL STRATEGIES

The radio partners offered volume-driving opportunities through the use of leveraged value-added remotes and promotions.

Locally, brand field specialists executed value-added events, grass-roots activity, field marketing, and public relations. Previously, local marketing and selling activity were sparse.

RESULTS

In summary, business growth for 1998 was projected at 25 percent. However . . .

Sales grew 56.7 percent in the Los Angeles Hispanic market (June-December, Nielsen 1998)

In 1998, Tecate® advanced to 8th-ranked imported beer in the U.S., from 11th in 1997 (Source: Impact Databank publication)

Tecate® became the number-two import in California (Nielsen, Dec. 1998)

CASE STUDY

United States Postal Service

THE SITUATION

Building on money order services, the U.S. Postal Service (USPS) developed a new product with improved security and faster delivery of cash outside the U.S. called Dinero Seguro®.

ELECTRONIC MONEY TRANSFER

Mexico was the first market targeted. Transactions from the U.S. to Mexico led the category with 65 percent of all wire transactions. Developed in alliance with Bancomer, a leading Mexican bank with the largest retail branch network, Dinero Seguro shared brand essence of security and reliability.

THE CHALLENGE

• Breaking into an established category.

• A highly competitive marketplace and extremely savvy consumers.

• Key competitors have long standing equity and spend aggressively in the category.

GOALS

• Leverage USPS's credibility and equity among the target audience.

• Create differentiation among electronic money transfer services.

• Use an integrated Hispanic communications plan to generate/build brand awareness, spur trial/retrial of Dinero Seguro.

POSITIONING STATEMENT

Dinero Seguro is fast, safe and the only service guaranteed by the U.S. Postal Service and Bancomer in Mexico that you can trust to electronically transfer your money to your loved ones in Mexico.

TARGET

Those who send money to their loved ones in Mexico. It is a moral and family obligation to send money back home on a regular basis. Two segments identified as greatest volume opportunities—groups made up primarily of Mexican immigrants including farm workers and blue collar workers, etc.

YOUNG & RUBICAM /THE BRAVO GROUP HISPANIC CAMPAIGN

Tan seguro como el amor de los suyos!

As sure/true as the love of your loved ones!

Campaign illustrates the closeness and emotional bond of immigrants in the U.S. and their family ties back home in Mexico. The struggle of the new immigrant in the U.S. is one of great pride and responsibility Sharing the fruits of their labor is important. Dinero Seguro helps to bridge this financial obligation.

INTEGRATED HISPANIC COMMUNICATIONS

Integrated Hispanic communications included:

Advertising: Generate/build brand awareness and drive trial/retrial

Promotions: Generate increased awareness, trial/retrial during high purchase opportunity periods

Event Marketing Build awareness, stimulate trial and drive traffic to post offices while creating goodwill

Direct Marketing: To stimulate and secure repeat purchase

CAMPAIGN RESULTS

Dinero Seguro meets and exceeds expectations, surpassing projected volume and revenue goals by over 35 percent.

• Brand awareness more than doubles.

• Advertising awareness almost triples.

• Total usage more than doubles.

• Key attributes increased at category leaders expense.

Received 1999 Gold Effie® Award in the Non-English Language category

SOURCES

CONSULTANTS

Cultural Access Group

5150 El Camino Real, Suite B-15

Los Altos, CA 94022

Tel: (650) 965-3859

Fax: (650) 965-3874

URL: www.accesscag.com

Type of Service: Bilingual and bicultural market research services. Has developed consumer studies and the Hispanic Household Panel in partnership with ACNielsen. The Panel reflects the demographic, cultural, and linguistic diversity of U.S. Hispanic consumers with complete purchase data.

Estrada Communications Group

633 W. Fifth St., Suite 1160

Los Angeles, CA 90071

Tel: (213) 623-2446

Fax: (508) 464-0246

URL: www.ESTRADAUSA.com

Type of Service: Public relations agency specializing in corporate marketing and communications.

Market Development Inc.

600 B St., Suite 1600

San Diego, CA 92101

Tel: (619) 232-5628

Fax: (619) 232-0373

URL: www.mktdev.com

Type of Service: MDI specializes in full-service qualitative and quantitative research

for the U.S. Hispanic market and Mexico. Custom research services include Spanish-language focus groups (in-house staff of bilingual moderators), concept testing, and consumer surveys. Standardized research services include: Consumer Linkage, a structured technique for generating advertising strategies; Hispanic Copy Trac, a quantitative copy-testing program for Spanish-language commercials. Also offered are Hispanic Omnibus and Hispanic Teen Omnibus, national surveys of the Hispanic market, conducted quarterly.

Erlich Transcultural Consultants

21241 Ventura Blvd., Suite 93

Woodland Hills, CA 91364

Tel: (818) 226-1333

Fax: (818) 226-1338

URL: www.etctranscultural.com

Type of service: This full-service company focuses its qualitative and quantitative marketing research efforts on Latinos, Asians, African Americans, and American Indians.

Findings International Corp.

9100 Coral Way, Suite 6

Miami, FL 33165

Tel: (305) 225-6517

Fax: (305) 225-6522

Type of service: Hispanic specialists. Complete range of qualitative and quantitative research and field services. Extensive experience not only in the United States but Central/South American and Caribbean markets. State-of-the-art facilities for the conduct of focus groups. Excellent recruiting capabilities. Experienced bilinguals to conduct telephone interviews.

Hispanic Marketing Communication Research

(A division of Hispanic & Asian Marketing Communication Research, Inc.)
1301 Shoreway Road, Suite 100
Belmont, CA 94002
Tel: (650) 595-5028
Fax: (650) 595-5407
URL: www.hamcr.com

Type of service: Qualitative and quantitative full-service research in English, Spanish and Portuguese in the United States and Latin America. Specializes in copy and execution testing, motivational discovery, perceptual positioning, product development, tracking, attitude and use studies, and cultural analysis for positioning products and services in diverse markets. Services include focus groups, one-on-ones, intercepts, video ethnographies, executive and business-to-business interviews, CATI surveys, multivariate design and statistical analysis.

RL Public Relations & Marketing

201 North Robertson Blvd., Suite A
Beverly Hill, CA 90211
Tel: (310) 385-1697
Fax: (310) 385-1698

Type of Service: Full service public relations and marketing organization dedicated to developing and executing breakthrough marketing communications programs for the Latino market in the U.S. and Latin America. The company provides expert marketing counsel that is both creative and results driven.

TGE Demographics Consulting

1244 Pittsford-Mendon Center Road
Honeoye Falls, NY 14472
Tel: (716) 624-7390
Fax: (716) 624-7394

Type of Service: Analysis and forecasting of demographics related to consumer markets.

NEWSLETTERS AND MAGAZINES

Marketing to the Emerging Minorities
EPM Publications
160 Mercer St., 3rd Floor
New York, NY 10012-3212
Tel: (212) 941-0099
Fax: (212) 941-1622
URL: www.epmcom.com

This newsletter covers black, Hispanic, Asian-American and other ethnic markets. Topics include family budgets; attitudes toward mainstream advertising, immigration and mobility; purchase decisions; demographics; and more. Annual subscription rate: $295 for 12 issues.

Multicultural Marketing News
Multicultural Marketing Resources, Inc.
286 Spring St., Suite 201
New York, NY 10003
Tel: (212) 242-3351
Fax: (212) 691-5969
URL: www.inforesources.com

This newsletter is published by Multicultural Marketing Resources, Inc., a public relations and marketing company specializing in promoting multicultural news. The bimonthly newsletter provides journalists with leads and story ideas and helps executives from business alliances. Each issue profiles 15 companies and provides a list of upcoming conferences and seminars. Annual subscription rate: $125. (*See also,* the SourceBook of Multicultural Experts, under *Directories* below.)

Hispanic Market Weekly
200 West 57th St., Suite 603
New York, NY 10019
Tel: (212) 333-7268

Fax: (212) 333-5385
URL: www.hmweekly.com

This newsletter covers agencies, advertisers, media and the people who move the Hispanic market. Published every Monday, the newsletter provides news, background, trends, and the numbers that affect the Hispanic advertising and media industries. Annual subscription rate: $247. Sample issues are available on the website.

Hispanic Business
425 Pine St.
Santa Barbara, CA 93117-3709
Tel: (805) 964-4554
Fax: (805) 964-6139
URL: www.hispanicbusiness.com

The magazine that covers Hispanic businesses and their owners as well as information useful to Hispanic business owners. Annually publishes lists of top-500 Hispanic-owned businesses, fastest-growing Hispanic high-tech businesses. Hispantelligence on web site is useful for market research. Annual subscription rate: $12.

Politico Magazine
1020 E. Mountain Vista Drive
Phoenix, AZ 85048
Tel: (480) 460-7646
Fax: (480) 460-5456
email: politicomkt@aol.com

News coverage, profiles, features and news analysis on Campaign 2000 and the influence of the Latino electorate. Also contains commentary, arts and culture, and a national calendar of events. Subscription rates: $36 a year; $20 for 6 months.

DIRECTORIES

Association of Hispanic Advertising Agencies

8201 Greensboro Drive

Mclean, VA 22102

Tel: (703) 610 9014

Fax: (703) 610 9005

URL: www.ahaa.org

AHAA produces an annual directory that lists all member agencies. Price is $39.95. It is updated in mid-year. The 2000 edition will be available in June or July.

Hispanic Media & Market Source

SRDS

1700 Higgins Road

Des Plaines, IL 60018-5605

Tel: (toll free) (800) 851-7737

Fax: (847) 375-5230

URL: www.srds.com

More than 1,700 listings of Hispanic radio, television, daily and weekly newspapers, consumer and business publications, outdoor advertising companies, direct mail advertising opportunities and special events. Organized by DMA and media type, Extensive roster of Hispanic suppliers and service providers. Issued 4 times a year. Annual subscription is $240.

Directory of National Association of Hispanic Publications

941 National Press Building

Washington, DC 20045

Tel: (202) 662-7250

Fax: (202) 662-7254

URL: www.nahp.org

Directory of Association members and their publications, issued annually. $95.

Hispanic Media Directory

3445 Catalina Drive

Carlsbad, CA 92008

Tel: (760) 434-7474

Fax: (760) 434-7476

Directory of the Latino Print Network which includes more than 160 publications in 50 markets. Information is published by market and publication, including frequency, circulation, language, publication dates, rates and more. Latin Print Network accepts advertising placements and consolidates billings. Annual convention in Las Vagas in the spring.

SourceBook of Multicultural Experts

286 Spring St., Suite 201

New York, NY 10013

Tel: (212) 242 3351

Fax: (212) 691-5969

URL: www.inforesources.com

Contains the names of more than 200 companies and individuals who specialize in some kind of multicultural market—including Hispanic, Asian-American, and African-American. Companies have paid to be included. Directory is $59.99 and is issued annually.

SELECTED NATIONAL ORGANIZATIONS

Association of Hispanic Advertising Agencies
8201 Greensboro Drive
Mclean, VA 22102
Tel: (703) 610-9014
Fax: (703) 610-9005
URL: www.ahaa.org

AHAA produces an annual directory that lists all member agencies. Price is $39.95. It is updated in mid-year. The 2000 edition will be available in June or July.

National Association of Latino Appointed and Elected Officials, Inc. (NALEO)
5800 S. Eastern Ave., Suite 365
Los Angeles, CA 90040
Tel: (323) 720-1932
Fax: (323) 720-9519
URL: www.naleo.org

NALEO encourages participation in the civic and governmental process by Latinos, and sponsors scholarships and conferences.

United States Hispanic Chamber of Commerce
1019 19th St. NW, Suite 200
Washington, DC 20036
Tel: (202) 842-1212
Fax: (202) 842 -3221
URL: www.ushcc.com

Founded in 1979, the USHCC aims to develop a business network to provide the Hispanic community with cohesion and strength. Through a network of nearly 200 Hispanic Chambers of Commerce and Hispanic business organizations, the USHCC communicates the needs and potential of Hispanic enterprise to the U.S. government and corporate America. The organization's web site includes many links to other Hispanic organizations and organizations that work with women in business.

WEB SITES

These web sites are noted not only for their research value, but also as a way to better understand Hispanic culture and as possible advertising vehicles. New Hispanic web sites are opening every day. The portals can often offer you links to other sites of interest.

Portals

www.Consejero.com	Timely news and community content in Spanish
www.latinolink.com	Hispanic population culture with interactive features
www.StarMedia.com	An all-purpose site that encompasses every subject
www.terra.com	A Spanish portal site opened in early 2000
www.ElSitio.com	South American website with many graphics
www.quepasa.com	Bilingual site with a menagerie of content and links
www.espanol.com	Mulitmedia created content and shopping site
www.Asociados.com	Country-specific content information

www.zonalatina.com	Media and marketing portal focusing on Latin America
www.latinos.com	Links to other Hispanic-related web sites

Research and Statistics

www.worldbank.org	The official site of World Bank that leads to data and information on South American and Caribbean countries
www.ntia.doc.gov	A U.S. government site that has marketing information by industry and country
www.forrester.com	The site for one of the leading researchers on web site use
www.nielsenmedia.com	Site of another leading media researcher, ACNielsen
www.statmarket.com	Site for statistics about the Internet and its users

Financial

www.ZonaFinanciera.com	In Spanish, information on investing
www.NetFuerza.com	In Spanish, multi-faceted information site
www.ccbn.com	CCBN is a leader in the rapidly emerging industry supporting essential communications between public companies and the investment community over the Internet

Marketing and Advertising

www.HispanicAd.com	News, information and resources about the Hispanic advertising and media industry
www.multiculturalresource.com	The online division of MTS, allows users to search for agencies based on multicultural criteria such as black, Asian-, or Hispanic-American specialization, together with other specifics such as location, size, or business experience
www.clicaqui.com	Bilingual website of Clica Qui, the company that represents many Hispanic-oriented web sites

Media

www.Entravision.com	Entravision Communications Company LLC was formed in 1996 to provide for the ownership and operation of a group of Spanish-language media outlets
www.Univision.com	Website for the Univision television network
www.hbcca.com	Hispanic Broadcasting Network focusing on radio
www.zspanish.com	Site of the Spanish Radio Network
www.urbanlatino.com	Combination magazine, music, and shopping site targeted to Latino youth, the Latino experience in the United States

www.laritmo.com	Latin-American rhythm magazine online
www.latinastyle.com	Culture, business and fashion for the contemporary Hispanic woman. Company is 100 percent Hispanic-owned.
www.latingirlmag.com	Magazine for Hispanic teenage girls
www.hispanicbusiness.com	Hispanic business magazine

Culture

www.soloella.com	Dedicated to the Spanish woman
www.am-latino.com	Direct links to Latino stars, personalities, and media
www.aplauso.com	New web site for Latin American cultural events, including children's theater.

Pharmaceutical/Health

www.familymeds.com	Health information and shopping for health items; bilingual
www.RX.com	Prescriptions and over the counter items
www.salud.com	Information on health issues and concerns in Spanish
www.graciasdoctor.com	Health information about Latin-American countries and the U.S. by country and topic; bilingual

E-Commerce

www.yavas.com	Latino books and music
www.mundonet.com	Merchandise related to soccer, home electronics, books, and music; bilingual
www.ethnicgrocer.com	Multicultural cuisine; foods from many nations
www.querico.com	Multicultural cuisine; groceries as well as music, health and beauty items from Argentina, Brazil, Mexico and the Caribbean
www.casademusica.com	Comprehensive source for Latin music from Z-Spanish Media Corporation
www.latinvision.com	Business network for sales and distribution of products between the United States and Latin-American countries

Careers

www.LatPro.com	Site for Hispanic professionals
www.Bilingual-jobs.com	Jobs and information for bilingual speakers
www.joblatino.com	Career information specifically for Latinos

ADVERTISING AGENCIES

This list is not inclusive, but represents some of the most active agencies in the Hispanic marketplace who are members of the American Association of Hispanic Advertising Agencies (ahaa).

Accentmarketing
800 Douglas Rd., Suite 100
Coral Gables, FL 33134
Tel: (305) 461-1112
Fax: (305) 461-0071
URL: www.accentmarketing.com

Acento Advertising
2048 Cotner Ave.
Los Angeles, CA 90025
Tel: (310) 479-8113
Fax: (310) 478-9541
URL: www.acento.com

Ad Américas Inc.
865 S. Figueroa St., 12th Floor
Los Angeles, CA 90017
Tel: (213) 688-7250
Fax: (213) 688-7295

al Punto Advertising, Inc.
730 El Camino Way, Suite 200
Tustin, CA 92780
Tel: (714) 544-0888
Fax: (714) 544-0830
URL: www.alpunto.com

Anita Santiago Advertising
2448 Main St.
Santa Monica, CA 90405
Tel: (310) 396-8846
Fax: (310) 392-8908

Anthony, Baradat, Iglesias Advertising
2601 S. Bayshore Dr., Suite 300 C
Miami, FL 33133
Tel: (305) 859-8989
Fax: (305) 859-8919
URL: www.abiadvertising.com

Arvizu Advertising & Promotions
3225 North Central, Suite 1600
Phoenix, AZ 85012
Tel: (602) 279-4669
Fax: (602) 279-4977
URL: www.arvizu.com

The Bravo Group
230 Park Avenue South, 9th Floor
New York, NY 10003
Tel: (212) 614-6001
Fax: (212) 598-5454
URL: www.yr.com/companies/bravo

Bromley, Aguilar & Associates
401 East Houston St.
San Antonio, TX 78205
Tel: (210) 244-2000
Fax: (210) 244-2400

BVK/Meka
848 Brickell Ave. #430
Miami, FL 33131
Tel: (305) 372-0028
Fax: (305) 372-0880
URL: www.bvk.com

Cartel Creativo Inc.
8627 Cinnamon Creek, Suite 501
San Antonio, TX 78240
Tel: (210) 696-1099
Fax: (210) 696-4299

Casanova Pendrill Publicidad, Inc.
3333 Michelson Dr., Suite 300
Irvine, CA 92612
Tel: (949) 474-5001
Fax: (949) 474-8424
URL: www.casanova.com

Castor Advertising Corporation
3 Park Ave., 35th Floor
New York, NY 10016
Tel: (212) 696-0990
Fax: (212) 696-5568
URL: www.castor-adv.com

Cohen Latino Communications
5111 Santa Fe St., Suite 223
San Diego, CA 92109
Tel: (858) 490-8660
Fax: (858) 490-8666
URL: www.cohenlatino.com

Conill Advertising
375 Hudson St., 8th Floor
New York, NY 10014
Tel: (212) 463-2500
Fax: (212) 463-2509

Creative Civilization–*An Aguilar Agency*
321 Alamo Plaza, Suite 200
San Antonio, TX 78205
Tel: (210) 227-1999
Fax: (210) 227-5999

cruz/kravetz: IDEAS
11400 W. Olympic Blvd., Suite 1700
Los Angeles, CA 90064
Tel: (310) 312-3630
Fax: (310) 312-9013
URL: www.ckideas.com

del Rivero Messianu Advertising
770 S. Dixie Hwy. #109
Coral Gables, FL 33146
Tel: (305) 666-2101
Fax: (305) 662-8043
URL: www.delriveromessianu.com

Dieste & Partners Publicidad
3102 Oak Lawn Blvd., Suite 109
Dallas, TX 75219
Tel: (214) 800-3500
Fax: (214) 800-3540
URL: www.dieste.com

Enlace Communications
11999 San Vicente Blvd. #345
Brentwood, CA 90049
Tel: (310) 440-5368
Fax: (310) 472-4099
URL: www.enlacecomm.com

Español Marketing & Communications
108 Turquoise Creek Dr., Suite C
Cary, NC 27513

Tel: (919) 462-8999
Fax: (919) 462-8009

Ethnic Marketing Group, Inc.
26074 Avenue Hall, Suite 20
Valencia, CA 91355
Tel: (661) 295-5704
Fax: (661) 295-5771

FOVA, INC.
Headquarters:
149 Madison Ave., 10th Floor
New York, NY 10016
Tel: (212) 686-2230
Fax: (212) 545-0883

West Coast Office:
6100 Wilshire Blvd., Suite 900
Los Angeles, CA 90048
Tel: (310) 936-4303
Fax: (310) 936-2792
URL: www.fovainc.com

Garcia/LKS
719 S. Flores St.
San Antonio, TX 78204
Tel: (210) 222-1591
Fax: (210) 222-9986
URL: www.garcialks.com

Grupo Cuatro Publicidad
3100 McKinnon, Suite 1100
Dallas, TX 75201-1046
Tel: (214) 871-2035
Fax: (214) 969-7017

HeadQuarters Advertising Inc.
221 Main St., Suite 920
San Francisco, CA 94105
Tel: (415) 777-4500
Fax: (415) 777-2117
URL: www.headquartersadv.com

Hernandez & Garcia LLC
7360 N. Lincoln Ave., Suite 100
Lincolnwood, IL 60712
Tel: (847) 676-4445
Fax: (847) 676-1420

IAC Advertising Group, Inc.
2725 SW 3rd Ave.
Miami, FL 33129
Tel: (305) 856-7474
Fax: (305) 856-2687
URL: www.iacadgroup.com

INVENTIVA, INC.
1777 N.E. Loop 410, Suite 911
San Antonio, TX 78217
Tel: (210) 826-1662
Fax: (210) 826-0178
URL: www.inventiva.com

International & Ethnic Communications
4609 Maryland Ave.
N. Minneapolis, MN 55428-5032
Tel: (612) 535-9572
Fax: (612) 535-9574
URL: www.intl-ethnic.com

JMCP Publicidad
110 5th Ave., 8th Floor
New York, NY 10011
Tel: (212) 463-1194
Fax: (212) 463-1190
URL: www.jmcp.com

La Agencia de Orcí
11620 Wilshire Blvd., 6th Floor
Los Angeles, CA 90025
Tel: (310) 444-7300
Fax: (310) 478-3587
URL: www.laagencia.com

Leo Burnett USA
35 W. Wacker Drive, 28th Floor
Chicago, IL 60601
Tel: (312) 220-5410
Fax: (312) 220-6212
URL: www.leoburnett.com

López Negrete Communications, Inc.
5615 Kirby Dr., Suite 250
Houston, TX 77098
Tel: (713) 877-8777
Fax: (713) 877-8796
URL: www.lopeznegrete.com

Lopito Ileana & Howie, Inc.
Metro Office Park
1st St., Bldg. 13
Guaynabo, PR 00968
Tel: (787) 783-1160
Fax: (787) 783-8063
URL: www.lih.com

Martí Flores Prieto & Wachtel-Hispanic
P.O. Box 2125
San Juan, PR 00922-2125
Tel: (787) 781-1616
Fax: (787) 277-1406
URL: www.mfpw.com

Mendoza-Dillon & Asociados
4100 Newport Place, Suite 600
Newport Beach, CA 92660
Tel: (714) 851-1811
Fax: (714) 851-249

Mendoza-Harmelin, Inc.
535 Righters Ferry Rd.
Bala Cynwyd, PA 19004
Tel: (610) 668-2700
Fax: (610) 668-8412
URL: www.Harmelin.com

Montemayor y Asociados
70 N.E. Loop 410
San Antonio, TX 78216
Tel: (210) 342-1990
Fax: (210) 525-1052

Premier Maldonado
815 N.W. 57th Ave., Suite 205
Miami, FL 33126
Tel: (305) 267-7737
Fax: (305) 267-7735
URL: www.pm-a.com

The San José Group
Advertising, Marketing & Public Relations
625 N. Michigan Ave., Suite 1601
Chicago, IL 60611
Tel: (312) 751-8500
Fax: (312) 751-9080
URL: www.thesanjosegroup.com

Sánchez & Levitan, Inc.
3191 Coral Way, Suite 510
Miami, FL 33145
Tel: (305) 442-1586
Fax: (305) 442-2598
URL: www.sanchezlevitan.com

Siboney USA–Dallas
3500 Maple Ave.
Dallas, TX 75219-3929
Tel: (214) 521-6060
Fax: (214) 521-6066
URL: www.siboneyusa.com

Siboney USA–Miami
1401 Brickell Ave., Suite 1100
Miami, FL 33131
Tel: (305) 373-2526
Fax: (305) 372-0206

Siboney USA–New York
40 West 23rd St., 6th Floor
New York, NY 10010-5201
Tel: (212) 337-8900
Fax: (212) 337-8901

Siboney USA–Los Angeles
4 Hutton Center Dr., Suite 900
Santa Ana, CA 92707-0505
Tel: (714) 979-6060
Fax: (714) 979-6228

The Vidal Partnership, Inc.
228 E. 45th St., 11th Floor
New York, NY 10017
Tel: (212) 867-5185
Fax: (212) 661-7650
URL: www.vidal-partnership.com

Zubi Advertising
3300 Ponce de Leon Blvd.
Coral Gables, FL 33134
Tel: (305) 448-9824
Fax: (305) 443-1573
URL: www.zubiad.com

LEADING HISPANIC BUSINESSES

Listed by 1998 turnover

MasTec Inc.
Miami, FL
CEO: Jorge Mas Jr.
Type of business: Telecommunications,
  infrastructure construction
No. of employees: 8,800
Year founded: 1969
Turnover 1998 (in millions): $1,005.10
Tel: (813) 626-2480

Burt Automotive Network
(Burt on Broadway)
Englewood, CO
CEO: Lloyd G. Chavez
Type of business: Automotive sales and
  service
No. of employees: 1,019
Year founded: 1939
Turnover 1998 (in millions): $837.53
Tel: (303) 761-0333

Goya Foods Inc.
Secaucus, NJ
CEO: Joseph A. Unanue
Type of business: Hispanic food manufac-
  turing and marketing
No. of employees: 2,200
Year founded: 1936
Turnover 1998 (in millions): $653.00
Tel: (201) 348-4900

Ancira Enterprises Inc.
San Antonio, TX
CEO: Ernesto Ancira Jr.
Type of business: Automotive sales and
  service
No. of employees: 550
Year founded: 1983
Turnover 1998 (in millions): $449.00
Tel: (210) 681-4900

International Bancshares Corp.
Laredo, TX
CEO: Dennis E. Nixon

Type of business: Financial services
No. of employees: 1,427
Year founded: 1965
Turnover 1998 (in millions): $367.87
Tel: (956) 722-7611

IFS Financial Corp.
Los Angeles, CA
CEO: Hugo Pimienta
Type of business: CA mortgage lending
  and insurance services
No. of employees: 2,100
Year founded: 1995
Turnover 1998 (in millions): $305.00
Tel: (310) 785-2100

Related Group of Florida
Miami, FL
CEO: Jorge M. Perez
Type of business: Real estate
  development
No. of employees: 200
Year founded: 1979
Turnover 1998 (in millions): $297.00
Tel: (305) 460-9900

Sedano's Supermarkets
Miami, FL
CEO: Manuel A. Herran
Type of business: Supermarket chain
No. of employees: 1,800
Year founded: 1962
Turnover 1998 (in millions): $294.00
Tel: (305) 554-8889

Troy Ford
Troy, MI
CEO: Irma B. Elder
Type of business: Automotive sales and
  service
No. of employees: 108
Year founded: 1967
Turnover 1998 (in millions): $291.65
Tel: (248) 585-4000

Lloyd A. Wise Cos.
Oakland, CA
CEO: Anthony A. Batarse Jr.
Type of business: Automotive sales and
  services
No. of employees: 222
Year founded: 1914
Turnover 1998 (in millions): $216.70
Tel: (510) 638-4800

Rosendin Electric Inc.
San Jose, CA
CEO: Raymond J. Rosendin
Type of business: Electrical contracting
No. of employees: 1,150
Year founded: 1919
Turnover 1998 (in millions): $206.00
Tel: (408) 286-2800

Supreme International Corp.
Miami, FL
CEO: George Feldenkreis
Type of business: Men's apparel design
  and wholesale
No. of employees: 368
Year founded: 1967
Turnover 1998 (in millions): $190.70
Tel: (305) 592-2830

AJ Contracting Company Inc.
New York, NY
CEO: Leonard Bass
Type of business: Construction
  management and contracting
No. of employees: 67
Year founded: 1917
Turnover 1998 (in millions): $183.18
Tel: (212) 889-9100

Mexican Industries in Michigan Inc.
Detroit, MI
CEO: Pamela A. Aguirre
Type of business: Automotive soft trim
  manufacturing
No. of employees: 1,453
Year founded: 1979
Turnover 1998 (in millions): $162.12
Tel: (313) 963-6114

Pan American Hospital
Miami, FL
CEO: Carolina Calderin
Type of business: Health-care services
No. of employees: 1,034
Year founded: 1963
Turnover 1998 (in millions): $156.00
Tel: (305) 264-1000

Precision Trading Corp.
Miami, FL
CEO: Israel Lapciuc
Type of business: Electric wholesale
No. of employees: 40
Year founded: 1979
Turnover 1998 (in millions): $155.00
Tel: (305) 592-4500

HUSCO International Inc.
Waukesha, WI
CEO: Agustin A. Ramirez
Type of business: Hydraulic controls man-
  ufacturer
No. of employees: 750
Year founded: 1985
Turnover 1998 (in millions): $150.00
Tel: (262) 547-0261

Avanti/Case-Hoyt
Miami, FL
CEO: Jose Arriola
Type of business: Commercial printing
  services
No. of employees: 1,000
Year founded: 1965
Turnover 1998 (in millions): $145.00
Tel: (305) 685-7381

Hamilton Bancorp Inc.
Miami, FL
CEO: Eduardo A. Masferrer
Type of business: Commercial banking
No. of employees: 265
Year founded: 1988
Turnover 1998 (in millions): $142.62
Tel: (305) 717-5500

McBride & Associates Inc.

Albuquerque, NM
CEO: Teresa McBride
Type of business: Computer products and services
No. of employees: 200
Year founded: 1986
Turnover 1998 (in millions): $140.00
Tel: (505) 883-0600

Lopez Foods Inc.

Oklahoma City, OK
CEO: John C. Lopez
Type of business: Meat products manufacturing
No. of employees: 313
Year founded: 1989
Turnover 1998 (in millions): $138.30
Tel: (405) 789-7500

Molina Medical Centers

Long Beach, CA
CEO: J. Mario Molina
Type of business: Health-care services
No. of employees: 433
Year founded: 1980
Turnover 1998 (in millions): $135.00
Tel: (562) 435-3666

Physicians Healthcare Plans Inc.

Coral Gables, FL
CEO: Miguel B. Fernandez
Type of business: Managed health-care services
No. of employees: 500
Year founded: 1993
Turnover 1998 (in millions): $131.00
Tel: (305) 441-9400

Complas Inc.

Corona, CA
CEO: Monica E. Garcia
Type of business: Telecommunications equipment and sales
No. of employees: 123
Year founded: 1989
Turnover 1998 (in millions): $130.00
Tel: (909) 371-5009

AIB Financial Group Inc.

Miami, FL
CEO: Jose M. "Pepe" Alvarez
Type of business: Full insurance services and brokerage
No. of employees: 413
Year founded: 1986
Turnover 1998 (in millions): $121.00
Tel: (305) 712-0000

Sales figures appear as reported to *Hispanic Business* by authorized company representatives. Many companies submitted financial statements.

BIBLIOGRAPHY

Many sources have been consulted to complete this volume. Among the most timeless and useful publications on the Hispanic population are the following. Please see also the list of resources which includes the U.S. Census Bureau and its myriad reports on Hispanic Americans.

Augenbraum, H. and Ilan Stavans, eds. *Growing Up Latino: Memories and Stories*. Boston: Houghton Mifflin, 1993.

Bachu, Amara. "Fertility of American Women: June 1995 (Update)," *Current Population Reports,* U.S. Bureau of the Census, October 1997.

Bean, Frank D., and Marta Tienda. *The Hispanic Population of the United States*. New York: Russell Sage Foundation, 1990.

Berry, J.W. "Acculturation and Adaptation in a New Society," *International Migration Quarterly Review* 30 (1992).

Biddlecom, A.E. and A.M. Hardy. "AIDS Knowledge and Attitudes of Hispanic Americans: United States, 1990." *Vital and Health Statistics,* Advanced Data No. 207. Hyattsville, MD: National Center for Health Statistics, 1991.

Braus, Patricia. "What Does Hispanic Mean?" *American Demographics*, Vol. 15, No. 6, (June 1993)

Bryson, Ken and Lynne M. Casper. "Household and Family Characteristics: March 1997," *Current Population Reports,* U.S. Bureau of the Census, March 1997.

Bronfenbenner, U. "Toward an Experimental Ecology of Human Development," *American Psychologist,* July 1977, 513–30.

Crispell, D., ed. "Pardon Me, Do You Speak English?" *American Demographics,* Vol. 12, No. 8, 1992.

Cultural Access Group and ACNielsen Homescan Consumer Panel, Hispanic Consumer*Facts, 1998.

de la Garza, Rodolfo O., Louis DeSipio, F. Chris Garcia, John Garcia, and Angelo Falcon. *Latino Voices: Mexican, Puerto Rican and Cuban Perspectives on American Politics*. Boulder, CO: Westview Press, 1992.

Edmonston, Barry, and Jeffrey S. Passel. "The Future Immigrant Population of the United States," Washington, DC: The Urban Institute, 1992.

Exter, T.G. "Consumer Household Projections by Age, Type of Household, Race, and Hispanic Origin 1990–2000." Ithaca, NY: TGE Demographics, 1992.

Falicov, Celia J. and Betty M. Karrer. "Cultural Variations in the Family Life Cycle: The Mexican American Family," in *Family Transitions: Continuity and Change over the Life Cycle,* ed. Celia J. Falicov. New York: Guilford Press, 1988.

Gil, Rosa Maria and Carman Vasquez. *The Maria Paradox: How Latinas Can Merge Old World Traditions with New World Self-esteem.* New York: G.P. Putnam's Sons, 1996.

Gordon, M. *Assimilation in American Life: The Role of Race, Religion, and National Origins.* New York: Oxford, 1964.

Hamburg, B.A. "Social Change and the Problems of Youth," in *American Handbook of Psychiatry,* 2nd ed. Ed. S. Ariefi. New York: Basic Books, 1975.

Holston, M. "Latino Beat," *Hispanic,* December 1992, 14–22.

Kanellos, Nicolas, ed. *The Hispanic-American Almanac: A Reference Work on Hispanics in the United States.* Detroit, MI: Gale Research, 1993.

Lappin, J. "On Becoming a Culturally Conscious Family Therapist," in *Cultural Perspectives in Family Therapy,* ed. J.C. Hanson and C.J. Falicov. Rockville, MD: Aspen Publications, 1979.

McGuill, D. "Cultural Concepts for Family Therapy," in *Cultural Perspectives in Family Therapy,* ed. J.C. Hanson and C.J. Falicov. Rockville, MD: Aspen Publications, 1983, 108–21.

Minuchin, S. and C. Fishman. *Family Therapy Techniques.* Cambridge, MA: Harvard University Press, 1981.

National Association of Latino Elected and Appointed Officials (NALEO) Educational Fund, The National Latino Immigrant Survey. Washington, DC: NALEO, 1989.

Ogilvy, David. *Confessions of an Advertising Man.* New York: Atheneum, 1963.

Overpeck, M.D. and A.J. Moss. "Children's Exposure to Environmental Cigarette Smoke Before and After Birth: Health of Our Nation's Children, United States 1998," *Vital and Health Statistics,* Advanced Data No. 202. Hyattsville, MD: National Center for Disease Control, 1991.

Paulin, Geoffrey D. "A Growing Market: Expenditures by Hispanic Consumers," *Monthly Labor Review,* Bureau of Labor Statistics, March 1998.

Selig Center for Economic Growth, University of Georgia, "Hispanic Buying Power by Place of Residence, 1990–1999," Nov-Dec. 1998.

Shick, L. and R. Shick, *Statistical Handbook on U.S. Hispanics.* Phoenix: Oryx Press, 1991.

Sosa, L. *The Americano Dream: How Latinos Can Achieve Success in Business and in Life.* New York: Penguin Group, 1998.

Theodorson, George A. and Achilles Theodorson. *A Modern Dictionary of Sociology.* New York: Thomas Y. Crowell Company, 1969.

The Tomas Rivera Policy Institute (TRPI). "Closing the Digital Divide: Enhancing Hispanic Participation in the Information Age," 1999.

Trompenaars, F. *Riding the Waves of Culture: Understanding Cultural Diversity in Global Business.* 2nd ed. New York: McGraw Hill, 1998.

INDEX